FRESHWATER GAMEFISH OF NORTH AMERICA

THE HUNTING & FISHING LIBRARY®

By Dick Sternberg

DICK STERNBERG'S experience as a fisheries biologist and fishing writer make him well qualified to author a book on North American freshwater gamefish. During production of this book, Dick fished throughout much of the United States, and in Canada and Alaska, personally catching almost 50 species of gamefish.

CY DE COSSE INCORPORATED
Chairman: Cy DeCosse
President: James B. Maus
Executive Vice President: William B. Jones

FRESHWATER GAMEFISH OF NORTH AMERICA
Author and Project Director: Dick Sternberg
Editor: Parker Bauer
Art Directors: Bradley Springer, William B. Jones
Principal Photographer: William Lindner
Technical Photo Director: Joseph Cella
Contributing Photographers: Christopher Batin; Erwin Bauer; Rudy Calin; Homer Circle; Dave Csanda; Abe Cuanang; Jack Ellis; Eric Gerstung; Daniel Halsey; Mike Hehner; Michael Jones; Ronald J. Keil; Tom McHugh/National Audubon Society, PR; Nebraska Game and Parks Commission; Oregon Historical Society; Jeff Rach; William Roston; Doug Stamm; Martin Strelneck; Gilbert van Ryckevorsel; Tim Whitney; Michael G. Wood.
Illustrations: Maynard Reece, Jon Q. Wright
Research: Mike Hehner, Eric Lindberg, Steven Lindberg, Dave McCormack, James Moynagh
Project Managers: Jan Baron, Teresa Marrone
Production Managers: Jim Bindas, Julie Churchill
Typesetting: Jennie Smith, Linda Schloegel
Production Staff: Janice Cauley, Joe Fahey, Carol Kevan, Yelena Konrardy, David Schelitzche, Nik Wogstad
Print Production Manager: Teresa Marrone

Contributors: Ralph Ashley; Dr. Reeve Bailey, University of Michigan; Ned Bass, Brady's Mountain Lodge; Bruce Bauer — Breedlove, Dennison, and Associates; Dr. Robert Behnke, Colorado State University; Marty Bell, Great Northern Whitewater Rafting; Dr. Robert Bellig, Gustavus Adolphus College; Don Brader, Arkansas Game and Fish Commission; Barry and Janet Brown, Clearwater West Resort; Elaine Chesser; Dick Christie, South Carolina Wildlife and Marine Resources Dept.; Pat Coffin, Nevada Dept. of Wildlife; Dick and Ruth Dienst, Ice Cracking Lodge; Bill Dougherty; Frankie Dusenka, Frankie's Live Bait; Dr. Robert Edwards, Pan American University; Dr. Jim Felley; Dr. Bud Freeman, University of Georgia; Chris Friese, Philadelphia Electric Company; Charles Frisbie, Maryland Dept. of Natural Resources; Butch Furtman; Gavins Point National Fish Hatchery — Fred Sayers, Clar Subeck; Georgia Dept. of Natural Resources — Russ Ober, Reggie Weaver; Dick Grzywinski; Pete Hill; Clark Hubbs, American Society of Icthyologists; Gary Hudson, Indiana Dept. of Natural Resources; Dean Hulverson; King Ko Inn — Mark Emery, Jay Hammond, Jon Vea; Jacques Leggett, Ministry of Environment and Parks, British Columbia; Dr. Eric Loudenslager, Humbolt State University; Dr. M. Scott Mettee, Alabama Geological Survey; Minnesota Dept. of Natural Resources — Eric Anderson, Darryl Bathel, Bruce Gilbertson, Jim Lilienthal, David Pederson, Duane Shodeen, John Spurrier, Dick Thompson, Don Woods; Nevada Dept. of Wildlife — Robert Layton, Mike Sevon; William L. Pflieger; Edwin Pister, California Dept. of Game and Fish; Dave Pritchard, Texas Parks and Wildlife; Jeff Rach; David Schleser, Dallas Aquarium; William D. Schmid; Harry Stiles; Dr. James Underhill, University of Minnesota; University of Florida — Dr. George Burgess, Dr. Carter Gilbert; Bill Vanderford; Virginia Dept. of Game and Inland Fisheries — Mitchell Norman, John Randolph, Ed Steinkoenig; Virginia Institute of Marine Science — Dr. Joe Loesch, Jim Owens; Chuck Wilbert; Dr. Tom Waters, University of Minnesota; Bryan Wilson; Michael G. Wood, Del Mar College; Charles Wooley; Troy Zakariasen
Cooperating Manufacturers: Alumacraft Boat Company — Roger McGregor; Arctic Cat Snowmobiles; Jim Bagley Bait Co.; Joe Bucher Tackle Co.; CarByDon Mfg. — Don Emitt; E-Z Loader Boat Trailers; Fenwick-Woodstream Corp.; Herrick Enterprises-Wave Wackers; HT Enterprises — Paul Grahl; Igloo Corporation — Jeff Goodrich; Jiffy Ice Augers/Feldmann Eng. & Mfg. Co., Inc.; Koden Electronics Co., Ltd. — Rod Romine; La Crosse Footwear, Inc.; Lightning Buoy, Inc.; Lowrance Electronics, Inc. — Thayne Smith; Lund American, Inc. — Jim Moore; Mercury Marine/Mariner Outboards — Stan Bular, Jim Kalkofen, Clem Koehler; Minn Kota Trolling Motors; Mister Twister, Inc. — Vince Vella; MotorGuide Trolling Motors; Nordic Crestliner Boat Company — Del Smith; Normark Corporation; Northland Tackle Company — John Peterson; Plano Tackle Boxes; Si-Tex Marine Electronics, Inc. — Dave Church, Jack Phillips; Stren Fishing Line; Strike Master, Inc.; Tommy Thompson Co.; Trilene Fishing Line; VMC, Inc.; Worth Manufacturing Company
Color Separations: Riverside Color Corp.
Printing: R. R. Donnelley & Sons Co. (1187)

Also available from the publisher: *The Art of Freshwater Fishing, Cleaning & Cooking Fish, Fishing With Live Bait, Largemouth Bass, Panfish, The Art of Hunting, Fishing With Artificial Lures, Walleye, Smallmouth Bass, Dressing & Cooking Wild Game.*

Library of Congress Catalog Card Number 87-24308
ISBN 0-86573-023-7

Distributed by Prentice Hall Press
A Division of Simon & Schuster, Inc., New York, NY
ISBN 0-13-331125-2

2

Contents

Introduction

This book is a complete reference guide to North American freshwater gamefish. It includes remarkable color photographs of every important freshwater gamefish species, along with a scientifically accurate text that explains complex biological information in easy-to-understand terms.

Author Dick Sternberg recognized the need for such a book during his days as a professional fisheries biologist. Hardly a day went by without a phone call from a fisherman having trouble identifying his catch. Anglers also called with questions on where to find specific kinds of fish, the best baits for different species, and how fast certain fish grow. One of the most common questions was, "Where can I buy a book with good pictures of fish?"

The books then available were either highly technical, or extremely basic. Very few of them contained information useful to fishermen. In most cases, the books had sketches of fish that bore little resemblance to real life. Or, they had black-and-white photos of preserved laboratory specimens. Seldom did the photos show the fish in their natural habitat. The books often had identification keys useful only to the reader willing to dissect the fish and examine its internal anatomy.

Freshwater Gamefish of North America was conceived, designed, and written with all of these concerns in mind. Sternberg combines his knowledge of fisheries biology and sportfishing with the latest in biological research to produce a fact-filled text with the kind of information fishermen want. In addition to pertinent biological facts, the text also includes information on sporting qualities, eating quality, and current world records.

The photographs of fish in their natural environment are unparalleled. Most were taken by Bill Lindner, one of the country's leading fish photographers. But photos of fish in their natural habitat may not show important identification features, so we included color illustrations by premier wildlife artists Maynard Reece and Jon Wright. Each species is shown in biologically accurate detail.

The book includes a chapter on each family of freshwater gamefish. Each chapter has a photo key to help you identify members of that family on the basis of external features. Photos show the important features much more clearly than the typical line drawings. Using these keys, you can accurately identify a fish at a glance rather than taking time to dissect it.

One of the problems in identifying fish is that many species have several similar forms. While most books include only the most common form, this volume discusses and provides illustrations of important subspecies, variants, and hybrids. It also explains how to differentiate between the sexes, in normal condition and at spawning time.

The main reason a book like this has never before been published is the difficulty and expense of photographing so many species in so many locations. Our film crew began their year-long challenge by filming lake trout in Ontario. They travelled to Florida and dozens of points in between to photograph sunfish, bass, and most other warmwater species. They finished by filming trout and salmon in Montana and Alaska. The result of their efforts is a book that will claim a prominent spot in your outdoor library.

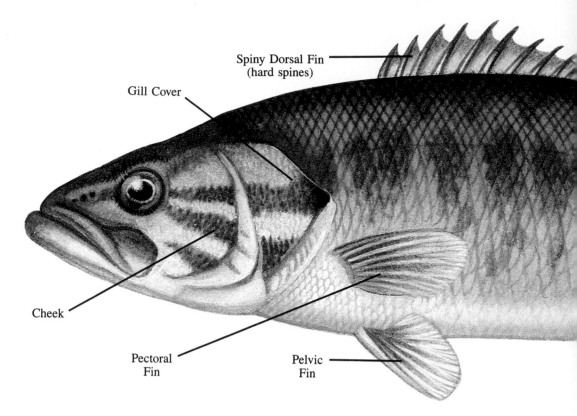

Spiny Dorsal Fin
(hard spines)

Gill Cover

Cheek

Pectoral
Fin

Pelvic
Fin

How to Use a Key

A key is a handy tool used by biologists to help identify various animals or plants. Keys identify anatomical features unique to a species so you can distinguish that species from other similar ones.

But most scientific keys are difficult for the average person to use. Certain anatomical features may not be apparent without dissecting the subject in question and examining its internal parts. Another problem with many keys: anatomical features are shown with line drawings that bear little resemblance to the features in real life.

The keys in this book were designed using external rather than internal features, all shown with high-quality color photography. This approach makes identification much easier. The trade-off is that external features may not be quite as reliable. A color bar, for instance, could be present on 95 percent of the subjects, but absent on 5 percent.

Anatomical features in the keys are normally listed in pairs, or couplets. Start with couplet 1. It will identify your fish, or instruct you to go to another couplet. Follow the instructions from couplet to couplet without bypassing any, until you find the one that identifies your fish.

If you know the family of a fish in question, but are uncertain of the species, go directly to the chapter on that family and refer to the species identification key. If you are not sure of the family, refer to the family identification key at right.

Family Identification Key

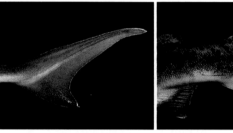

1 *Spine extends into upper lobe of tail* . . . . *go to* **2**   *Spine ends at base of tail* . . . *go to* **3**

4 Skin with scales . . . . . .
SALMON (pp. 8-55)   Skin without scales . . . . . .
CATFISH (pp. 110-127)

7 2 anal spines . . . .
PERCH (pp. 102-109)   *3 or more anal spines* . . . . .
go to **8**

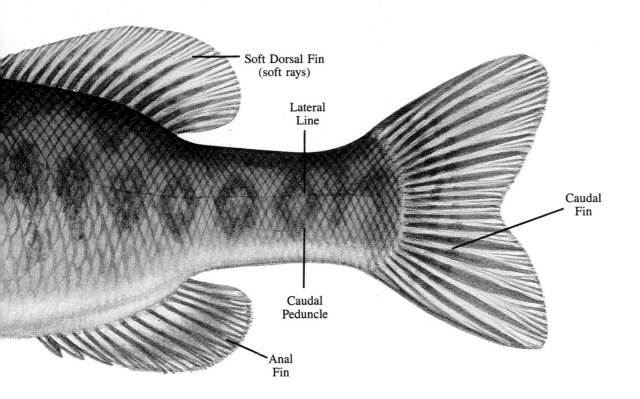

Soft Dorsal Fin
(soft rays)

Lateral
Line

Caudal
Fin

Caudal
Peduncle

Anal
Fin

2 Long, paddle-like snout . . . PADDLEFISH (pp. 128-131)   Shorter snout with barbels . . STURGEON (pp. 128-137)

3 *Adipose fin (arrow) present* . . . . *go to* **4**
No adipose fin . . . . *go to* **5**

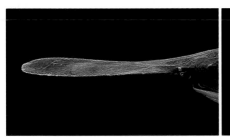

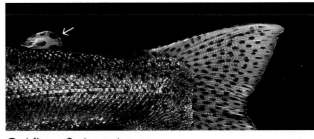

5 *Lateral line present* . . . . *go to* **6**   No lateral line . . . . HERRING (pp. 148-153)

6 Long jaws, shaped like duck's bill . . PIKE (pp. 92-101)
Shorter jaws . . . . *go to* **7**

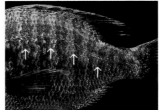

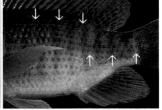

8 Sharp spine (arrow) at rear of gill cover . . . . . TEMPERATE BASS (pp. 138-147)   *No sharp spine at rear of gill cover* . . . . *go to* **9**

9 Lateral line (arrows) complete . . . . SUNFISH (pp. 56-91)   Lateral line (arrows) broken . . . . CICHLID (pp. 154-155)

Salmon Family

The family *Salmonidae* is a widespread group of coldwater fish that are commonly referred to as salmonids. It includes the following three subfamilies: salmon, trout and char; whitefish; and grayling.

SALMON, TROUT AND CHAR. These are perhaps the most highly esteemed of all gamefish. Strong fighters, they can be taken by fly fishing; casting or trolling with spoons, spinners and small plugs; and fishing with live bait. The table quality of most of these fish is excellent.

Salmon are *anadromous* fish, spending most of their life at sea, then returning to fresh water to spawn. But many species of salmon, including

Spawning male sockeye salmon — Dumpling Creek, Alaska

chinook, coho, sockeye and Atlantic, have been successfully stocked in freshwater lakes. Pacific salmon (genus *Oncorhynchus*) die shortly after spawning; Atlantic salmon do not. Atlantic salmon are more closely related to trout, and may live to spawn two or more times.

Trout and char are primarily freshwater fish, but many species develop seagoing races or subspecies. Brooks, rainbows, browns and cutthroats have anad-

romous forms that look different than the freshwater forms. Anadromous forms are sleeker, more silvery and usually lack distinctive coloration. One species, the Arctic char, is much like a salmon, spending the majority of its life at sea. And like many salmon, they are found in some freshwater lakes.

Trout (genus *Salmo*) differ from char (genus *Salvelinus*) because of their preference for warmer water. Trout have dark spots on a light background; char, light spots on a dark background. Some species, although called trout, are actually char. These include lake trout, brook trout and bull trout.

Because of their tremendous popularity, salmon, trout and char have been stocked widely throughout North America, probably more widely than any other group of fish. Beginning in the late 1800s, the U.S. Fish Commission planted them in virtually any type of water that could be reached by rail. A few of these introductions were successful; most were not.

As biologists learned more about the habitat requirements of these fish, stocking became more successful. Today, such stocking is a major part of the fish management program in many states.

Before this widespread stocking began, there were many different genetic variations within most of the major trout and char species. Many of these variants have been lost by mixing of genetically different stocks, but some still exist. We will discuss only those varieties and subspecies that still support significant sport fisheries.

Salmon Family — Species Identification Key

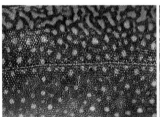

1 Base of dorsal fin at least as long as head . . GRAYLING
Base of dorsal fin shorter than head . . . . *go to 2*

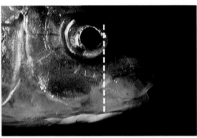

2 *Jaw extends beyond center of eye* . . . . . . *go to 5*   *Jaw not extending beyond center of eye (Whitefish)* . . . *go to 3*

5 *Anal fin no longer than deep* . . . . *go to 8*   *Anal fin longer than deep (Pacific Salmon)* . . . *go to 6*

6 Large black spots over entire tail . . . .
PINK SALMON   Small black spots over entire tail . . . .
CHINOOK SALMON

 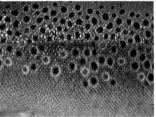

8 *Light spots on dark background (Char)* . . . .
go to 13   *Dark spots on light background (Trout and Atlantic Salmon)* . . . . *go to 9*

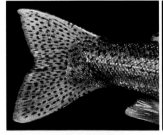 

9 *Tail with radiating rows of black spots* . . . *go to 10*   *Tail with few or no spots* . . . .
go to 12

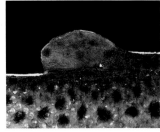 

12 Adipose fin with spots
BROWN TROUT   Adipose fin without spots . . .
ATLANTIC SALMON

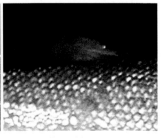

13 Tail deeply forked . . .
LAKE TROUT
Tail slightly forked or square . .
go to 14   **14** Wormlike marks on back
BROOK TROUT
No wormlike marks . . . . . .
go to 15

WHITEFISH. The whitefish group includes a wide variety of chubs, bloaters and other small fish with little sportfishing value. But anglers are discovering that some of the larger members of the group, such as lake whitefish, mountain whitefish and ciscoes, offer excellent fishing opportunities.

One member of the whitefish group, the inconnu, is anadromous. All others are restricted to fresh water. Most whitefish are plankton eaters; only the inconnu is primarily a fish eater. But those that eat plankton can be caught on hook and line by using very small baits and lures. They rise to an artificial fly, and some can even be caught by ice fishing with teardrop jigs baited with insect larvae.

GRAYLING. Only one species of grayling, the Arctic grayling, is found in North American waters. It can easily be identified by the large, sail-like dorsal fin. Grayling are common in remote areas of Alaska and northern Canada, and have been stocked in some northern states. But they are easily caught on hook and line, so populations are quickly depleted in areas with heavy fishing pressure.

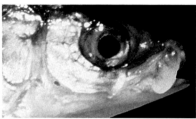

3 Jaws of equal length. . . . **CISCO**   Lower jaw projects beyond upper jaw . . . **INCONNU**
Upper jaw projects beyond lower jaw . . . . *go to 4*

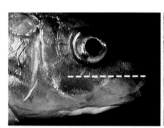
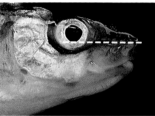

4 Tip of snout below lower margin of eye . . . . **MOUNTAIN WHITEFISH**   Tip of snout above lower margin of eye . . . . **LAKE WHITEFISH**

Small black spots on upper lobe of tail only . . . . **COHO SALMON**   *Tail without spots* . . . . *go to 7*

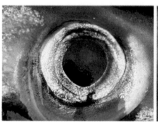

7 Pupil large, more than half the diameter of entire eye **CHUM SALMON**   Pupil small, less than half the diameter of entire eye . . . . . **SOCKEYE SALMON**

10 White margin on dorsal, anal and pelvic fins . . **GOLDEN TROUT**
No white margins on fins . . . *go to 11*

11 Reddish slash marks on throat . . . **CUTTHROAT TROUT**   No reddish slash marks . . . . **RAINBOW TROUT**

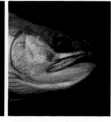

15 Long, broad, flat head . . **BULL TROUT**   *Shorter, narrower, rounder head* . . . . *go to 16*

16 Largest spots smaller than pupil of eye . . . . **DOLLY VARDEN**   Largest spots at least as large as pupil of eye . . . . **ARCTIC CHAR**

Arctic Grayling *(Thymallus arcticus)*

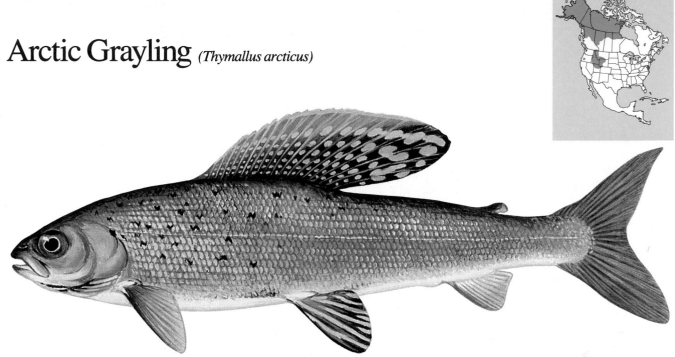

MALE GRAYLING — Long dorsal fin; when depressed, it extends to or nearly to the adipose fin.

Common Names — American grayling, bluefish, Arctic trout, sailfin, tittimeg. The name *thymallus* refers to the faint aroma of thyme given off by freshly caught grayling.

Description — Large dorsal fin, its base at least as long as the head. Dorsal is dark gray, with rows of blue or violet spots. Pelvic fins have distinct light streaks. Body iridescent violet-gray and silver, with small spots. In streams, grayling tend to take on the color of the bottom.

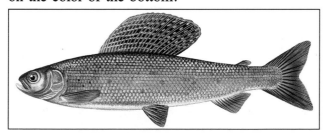

FEMALE GRAYLING — Dorsal fin shorter than that of male; when depressed, it does not extend to the adipose fin.

Table Quality — Excellent eating; flaky, white meat not as oily as that of most other salmonids.

Sporting Qualities — Quick to take a fly and likely to jump when hooked. Easy to catch with wet or dry flies, nymphs, small spinning lures and natural bait, especially salmon eggs. Grayling have strong schooling tendencies.

Habitat — Cold, clear, unpolluted waters of large rivers, rocky creeks and oligotrophic lakes. Seldom found in deep water. Preferred water temperature: 42° to 50°F.

Food Habits — Feed primarily on insects and salmon eggs; they occasionally eat molluscs, crustaceans and small fish.

Spawning Habits — Spawn in small streams during spring break-up, usually at water temperatures of 44° to 50°F. They prefer gravel- or rock-bottomed tributaries of lakes and larger streams. Parents do not build a redd or care for eggs or young.

Age and Growth — Maximum life span 10 years; very slow-growing and late to mature. Males usually grow faster than females. Two- to three-pounders commonly taken in Alaska and northern Canada; seldom exceed 1 pound in western U.S.

Typical Length (inches) at Various Ages

Age	1	2	3	4	5	6	7	8	9
Length	6.3	9.6	10.6	12.4	14.5	15.5	16.8	17.3	17.8

Typical Weight (pounds) at Various Lengths (inches)

Length	8	10	12	14	16	18	20
Weight	.20	.28	.52	.93	1.3	1.9	2.9

World Record — 5 pounds, 15 ounces, caught in the Katseyedie River, Northwest Territories, in 1967.

18-inch male grayling — Naknek River, Alaska

Mountain Whitefish *(Prosopium williamsoni)*

Mountain whitefish — South Fork, Flathead River, Montana

Common Names — Whitefish, Rocky Mountain whitefish.

Description — Slender, cylindrical body with small head, silvery sides and coarse scales. Mouth underslung; snout below level of eye.

Table Quality — The oily meat is good when eaten fresh, and is excellent when smoked.

Sporting Qualities — Good fighters, mountain whitefish can be caught on flies and natural bait. They bite especially well during the winter months. But many anglers consider them rough fish because they compete with trout.

Habitat — Prefer pools and slow-moving stretches of coldwater streams. Also found in the depths of oligotrophic lakes. They often occupy the same habitat as trout. Preferred water temperature: 46° to 52°F.

Food Habits — Feed mainly on bottom organisms, including immature insects and crustaceans. They will also take insects on the surface.

Spawning Habits — Spawn in late fall or early winter, usually at water temperatures of 42°F or less. Spawning normally takes place in gravelly stream riffles, but sometimes in lakes. Mountain whitefish do not build a redd or attempt to guard the eggs. The eggs incubate over winter and hatch in spring.

Age and Growth — Grow slowly but may live up to 18 years. Fish caught by anglers normally weigh 1 to 2 pounds.

Typical Length (inches) at Various Ages

Age	1	2	3	4	5	6	7	8	9
Length	5.8	8.4	9.6	10.6	11.3	12.3	13.1	14.0	15.0

Typical Weight (pounds) at Various Lengths (inches)

Length	11	12	13	14	15	16	17
Weight	.27	.57	.73	.86	1.1	1.3	1.6

World Record — 5 pounds, 2 ounces, caught in the Columbia River, Washington, in 1983.

Lake Whitefish *(Coregonus clupeaformis)*

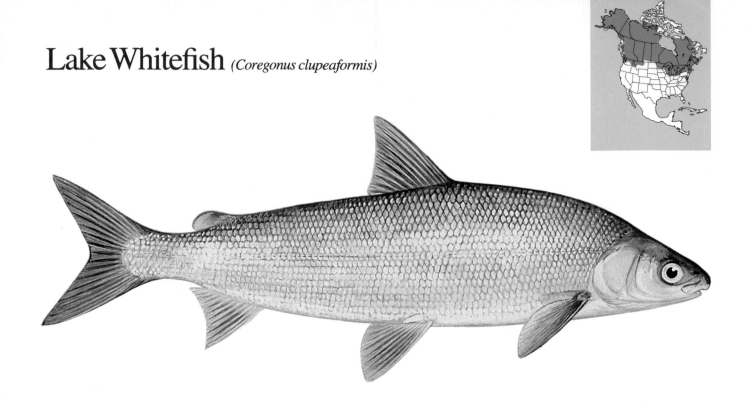

Common Names — Common whitefish, Great Lakes whitefish, Sault whitefish, humpback whitefish.

Description — Silvery sides with large scales and no markings. Body more laterally compressed than that of mountain whitefish; snout more underslung than that of cisco.

Forms — This is a very "plastic" species, with different populations taking on slightly different appearances. There are no generally recognized subspecies, but dwarf forms occur in some northern lakes.

Hybrids — In the Great Lakes, lake whitefish sometimes hybridize with ciscoes to produce a cross called mule whitefish, which grow faster and are a much brighter green than either of the parents. Lake whitefish also hybridize with inconnu.

Table Quality — Lake whitefish are the most important commercial species in Canada. The flesh is oily but has an excellent flavor. They are popular both fresh and smoked.

Sporting Qualities — Although they are not the best fighters, lake whitefish are becoming more popular, especially with ice fishermen. They can be caught on small minnows, either live or salted; teardrop jigs baited with waxworms; and small jigging lures. They respond well to chum. On calm summer mornings and evenings, whitefish feed on the surface and can be taken with flies.

Habitat — Found in the cold depths of oligotrophic lakes, often with lake trout. In Lake Superior, they have been taken in nets at depths as great as 420 feet. In the far North, they can survive in shallow lakes. They prefer water temperatures of 50° to 55°F.

Food Habits — Primarily bottom feeders, they eat insect larvae, molluscs, fish eggs and small fish. But during a hatch, they can often be seen taking insects on the surface.

Spawning Habits — Spawn in late fall or early winter, usually on shoal areas of large lakes, but occasionally in tributary streams. Spawning begins at a water temperature of about 43°F. Lake whitefish do not build nests. The eggs incubate over winter and hatch the following spring.

Age and Growth — Like mountain whitefish, lake whitefish have a maximum life span of about 18 years. But the growth rate is faster, so they reach a much larger size.

Typical Length (inches) at Various Ages

Age	1	3	5	8	11	14	17
North	5.8	8.8	11.0	17.0	17.5	21.0	23.4
South	9.2	15.9	18.0	18.7	20.6	21.4	24.3

Typical Weight (pounds) at Various Lengths (inches)

Length	12	14	16	18	20	22	24	26
Weight	.9	1.4	1.9	2.6	3.4	4.1	5.0	6.2

World Record — 14 pounds, 6 ounces, caught in Lake Huron near Meaford, Ontario, in 1984. Much larger whitefish have been taken in nets, including a 42-pounder caught in Lake Superior in 1918.

Whitefish taken in commercial nets — Apostle Islands, Lake Superior

Cisco *(Coregonus artedii)*

Common Names — Tullibee, herring, lake herring.

Description — Silvery sides with a faint pink or purple iridescent sheen. The upper and lower jaws are equal in length, so the mouth is at the tip of the snout. Ciscoes resemble American shad and other members of the herring family, accounting for some of their regional names. But unlike herring, ciscoes have an adipose fin.

Forms — The cisco's size and shape vary greatly from one body of water to another. Some northern lakes support a dwarf form. At one time, as many as 24 subspecies were recognized, but most taxonomists now recognize none.

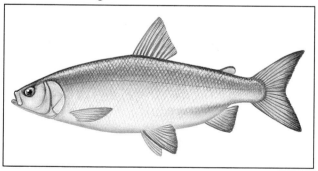

TULLIBEE — The body is considerably deeper than that of an ordinary cisco. Most common in mesotrophic lakes.

Hybrids — Ciscoes hybridize with lake whitefish, inconnu and other closely related fishes like the round whitefish and bloater.

Table Quality — The white meat is oily, but excellent when smoked. In some waters, however, the flesh is heavily infested with tapeworm larvae.

Sporting Qualities — When ciscoes are taking mayflies on the surface, they can easily be caught on flies. Ice fishing for ciscoes is becoming more popular in many areas. The usual bait is a teardrop

jig baited with a grub, but some are caught on small minnows. Ciscoes are not strong fighters.

Habitat — Found mainly in deep, cold, oligotrophic lakes, but can survive in mesotrophic lakes with adequate oxygen in the depths. They inhabit some rivers in the far North. Ciscoes do not relate to any particular type of bottom, but are constantly on the move in search of plankton. In summer, they normally cruise just below the thermocline, but will come to the surface in the morning and evening to feed on insects. They prefer a water temperature of about 55°F.

Food Habits — Primarily plankton feeders, ciscoes will also eat fish eggs and fry, small crustaceans, and a variety of adult and larval insects.

Spawning Habits — Spawn in fall when water temperatures are dropping. Spawning activity begins at about 40°F and peaks at about 38°. Ciscoes spawn a week or two later than lake whitefish. They scatter their eggs over a rock or gravel bottom, then abandon them. The eggs hatch the following spring.

Age and Growth — Ciscoes have been known to live as long as 13 years, but few live longer than 8. Males and females grow at about the same rate, but females live longer.

Typical Length (inches) at Various Ages

Age	1	2	3	4	5	6	7	8	9
Cisco	6.1	8.2	10.4	11.3	11.9	12.2	13.5	13.9	14.7
Tullibee	8.3	10.4	12.4	13.6	14.4	15.3	15.7	16.2	16.7

Typical Weight (pounds) at Various Lengths (inches)

Length	10	11	12	13	14	15	16	17
Cisco	.27	.35	.45	.57	.71	.86	1.0	—
Tullibee	.42	.58	.77	.99	1.3	1.6	1.9	2.3

World Record — 7 pounds, 6 ounces, caught in Cedar Lake, Manitoba, in 1986.

16- to 18-inch ciscoes — Mille Lacs Lake, Minnesota

Inconnu *(Stenodus leucichthys)*

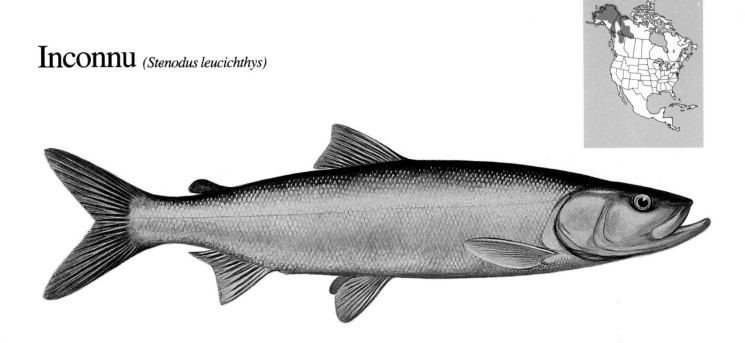

Common Names — Sheefish, conny, Eskimo tarpon, shovelnose whitefish.

Description — Overall silvery coloration; small teeth on upper and lower jaw and on roof of mouth; lower jaw projects beyond upper.

Subspecies — Although there are two subspecies of inconnu, only one is found in North America. The other is found near the Caspian Sea.

Hybrids — Inconnu occasionally hybridize with ciscoes and lake whitefish.

Table Quality — Oily flesh; tastes best when smoked, but can be eaten fresh.

Sporting Qualities — Easily caught during the downstream migration in fall. Best lures are spoons and small spinners, but inconnu will take streamers. Small inconnu tend to leap when hooked, accounting for the name "Eskimo tarpon"; big ones make deep, powerful runs.

Habitat — Inconnu are anadromous in coastal rivers, but are also found in oligotrophic lakes. Lake-dwelling inconnu migrate up tributary streams in summer (probably a spawning run), and return to the lake in late fall. Inconnu prefer water temperatures from 48° to 50°F.

Food Habits — The diet consists almost entirely of small fish, at times including northern pike, salmon, and even their own young.

Spawning Habits — Spawn in fall in rivers, beginning when water temperatures drop to the upper 30s. They do not build redds, but scatter the eggs over rubble where they sink into the crevices. An individual inconnu spawns only once every 3 to 4 years.

Age and Growth — Maximum age is probably about 20 years, although few live longer than 13. Because of their predatory habits, they grow faster than any other type of whitefish. The average inconnu weighs 5 to 10 pounds.

Typical Length (inches) at Various Ages

Age	1	3	5	7	9	11	13	15	17
Length	6.8	14.7	19.3	24.6	31.2	34.4	37.2	40.6	43.9

Typical Weight (pounds) at Various Lengths (inches)

Length	10	15	20	25	30	35	40	45
Weight	.42	1.2	3.0	7.4	10.7	12.3	19.1	28.5

World Record — 53 pounds, caught in the Pah River, Alaska, in 1986. Unofficially, a 63-pounder was caught at the mouth of the Mackenzie River, Northwest Territories, in 1936.

30-pound inconnu — Kobuk River, Alaska

Pink Salmon *(Oncorhynchus gorbuscha)*

Common Names — Humpback salmon, humpy, autumn salmon.

Description — Silvery sides; the upper sides, back, and both lobes of the tail have large black spots, some as large as the eye.

Hybrids — Known to hybridize with chum salmon.

Table Quality — The pinkish flesh is considered good eating, but not as good as that of sockeye, coho or chinook.

Sporting Qualities — Because of their preference for small food items, pink salmon may be difficult to catch on hook and line. In most coastal streams,

Spawning female (foreground) and spawning male (background) — Poplar River, Minnesota, a tributary to Lake Superior

they run late in the season when few fishermen are around. They can be taken on small spinning lures and yarn flies prior to the spawning run. After the run begins, the flesh deteriorates quickly, so the fish have little food value.

Habitat — Primarily an anadromous fish that enters streams along the Pacific coast to spawn. Accidentally introduced into Lake Superior in 1956, pinks have now spread into the other Great Lakes, and their numbers are rapidly increasing. They prefer water temperatures from 52° to 57°F.

Food Habits — At sea, pink salmon eat plankton, crustaceans, squid and small fish. They do not feed in the streams.

Spawning Habits — Spawn in early to late fall in coastal rivers, or in streams tributary to the upper Great Lakes. Usual water temperatures at spawning time are 43° to 48°F. Pinks migrate only a short distance upstream. Females dig a series of redds in gravel riffles. While the females are digging, the males fight savagely among themselves, sometimes inflicting deep wounds with their large canine teeth.

Most pinks spawn at age 2; only a few spawn at age 3. Both sexes die soon after spawning. Because of the definite two-year life cycle, spawning runs tend to be heavier in alternate years.

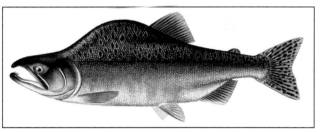

SPAWNING MALE PINK SALMON — Tremendous hump in front of dorsal fin, hooked upper jaw, prominent kype, large canine teeth. Sides usually brownish to olive and may be tinged with red or yellow. Spawning females have similar coloration.

Age and Growth — Because of their short life span, pinks do not grow as large as other Pacific salmon. Sea-run pinks average 3 to 5 pounds; Great Lakes pinks, only 1 to 2 pounds.

Typical Length (inches) at Various Ages

Age	1	2	3
Sea-run	13.2	24.0	—
Great Lakes	8.4	15.7	19.3

Typical Weight (pounds) at Various Lengths (inches)

Length	14	16	18	20	22	24
Weight	1.1	1.5	1.9	2.4	3.2	4.2

World Record — 12 pounds, 9 ounces, caught at the confluence of the Moose and Kenai rivers, Alaska, in 1974.

Chinook Salmon *(Oncorhynchus tshawytscha)*

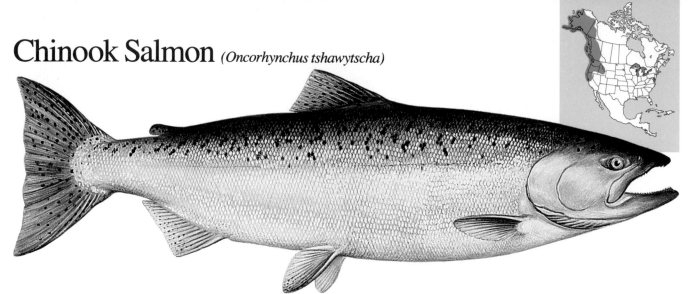

Common Names — King salmon, spring salmon, tyee, quinnat, blackmouth and blackjaw.

Description — Silvery sides with small dark spots on back and both lobes of tail. Teeth set in black gums (photo at right). Lower jaw comes to a sharp point.

Hybrids — Known to hybridize with coho salmon.

Table Quality — The flesh is reddish to white, with the reddish flesh commanding a higher price at the market. Considered one of the most delicious of the Pacific salmon.

Sporting Qualities — An extremely strong fighter, it may strip off 200 to 300 yards of line on its initial run. Then, it sounds and refuses to come in. A 30-pounder can easily wage a half-hour battle. Chinooks are extremely wary and sensitive to light. They are not as likely to feed on the surface as cohos. Effective lures include plugs with an erratic action, spoons and trolling flies. Chinooks also bite on whole or cut baitfish, and on spinner-salmon egg combinations.

Habitat — Anadromous, entering Pacific coastal streams, especially large ones, to spawn. Stocked in many inland lakes, including the Great Lakes and reservoirs on the upper Missouri River. Preferred water temperature: 53° to 57°F.

Food Habits — Fish make up most of the diet, but chinooks also eat squid, shrimp, crab larvae and other crustaceans.

Spawning Habits — Chinooks are strong swimmers and excellent leapers, so they move long distances upstream to spawn, sometimes as far as 1500 miles. Many streams have spring and fall runs. Spring chinooks stay in the river through the summer and spawn in early fall. Fall chinooks enter the river later and spawn later. Chinooks spawn in deeper water and on larger gravel than other Pacific salmon. Spawning takes place at water temperatures from 40° to 55°F.

The female builds a large redd, sometimes as much as 12 feet long and a foot deep. She is attended by one large, dominant male and by several younger males, or *jacks*. After spawning, the female guards the nest for a few days to two weeks, then dies. The jacks may survive for several months. Spawning is seldom successful in Great Lakes tributaries.

SPAWNING MALE CHINOOK — Strongly hooked upper jaw, prominent kype, very large canine teeth, and no hump on the back. Sea-run fish have reddish to pinkish brown sides; Great Lakes fish (shown above), olive to dark brown sides. Spawning females have similar coloration.

Age and Growth — Chinook spawn at age 2 to 9, usually age 4. Both sexes, including the jacks, die after spawning. An average adult chinook weighs 15 to 25 pounds, with males usually attaining the greatest weights.

Typical Length (inches) at Various Ages

Age	1	2	3	4	5	6
Sea-run	3.2	16.6	27.3	35.8	41.9	45.7
Great Lakes	10.7	18.6	26.9	33.2	38.6	—

Typical Weight (pounds) at Various Lengths (inches)

Length	21	24	27	30	33	36	39	42	45
Weight	3.9	5.9	8.6	12.0	16.3	21.5	27.7	34.9	43.5

World Record — 97 pounds, 4 ounces, caught in the Kenai River, Alaska, in 1985. Chinooks as large as 126 pounds have been taken by commercial fishermen.

38-pound bright female chinook — Naknek River, Alaska

Coho Salmon *(Oncorhynchus kisutch)*

Common Names — Silver salmon, blueback.

Description — Silvery sides with bluish or greenish back. Small black spots on the sides and back, and on the upper lobe of the tail. Teeth set in whitish to grayish gums (photo at right). Lower jaw blunter than that of chinook.

Hybrids — Known to hybridize with chinook.

Table Quality — Excellent. Some regard the reddish flesh as even better eating than that of chinook or sockeye.

Sporting Qualities — Considered by many anglers the most sporting of all the Pacific salmon. Cohos

11-pound bright male coho — Naknek River, Alaska

are usually caught near the surface and leap repeatedly. They can change direction so fast that fishermen mistakenly assume they have thrown the hook. Cohos can be caught with spoons, spinners, plugs, dodger-fly combinations and spawn bags.

Habitat — Anadromous, spawning in many small streams and some large ones along the Pacific coast. Introduced into many inland lakes including the Great Lakes and upper Missouri River reservoirs. Preferred water temperature: 53° to 57°F.

Food Habits — The diet consists mainly of fish, sometimes including young pink and chum salmon. Cohos also eat a variety of crustaceans. In the Great Lakes, alewives are the primary food.

Spawning Habits — Cohos run in mid- to late fall, usually later than other Pacific salmon. In small rivers, they swim farther upstream than pink, chum or sockeye salmon. The female digs redds in shallow gravel riffles with swift water. She is attended by a large, dominant male and several jacks. Spawning normally occurs at water temperatures of 46° to 52°F. After spawning, the female guards the nest for several days, then dies. Spawning in Great Lakes tributaries is seldom successful, although there has been some reproduction in tributaries of Lake Superior.

SPAWNING MALE COHO — Thick, strongly hooked upper jaw; well-developed kype; large canine teeth; and no hump on the back. Sea-run fish have greenish head and bright red sides; Great Lakes fish (shown above), grayish to greenish head and sides, usually with reddish lateral band. Spawning females have similar coloration.

Age and Growth — Cohos spawn at age 2 to 5, most commonly at age 3. Both sexes die after spawning. Males generally weigh more than females.

Typical Length (inches) at Various Ages

Age	1	2	3
Sea-run	5.7	12.2	27.4
Great Lakes	5.3	14.7	24.9

Typical Weight (pounds) at Various Lengths (inches)

Length	16	18	20	22	24	26	28	30
Weight	1.4	2.0	2.8	3.8	5.0	6.4	8.1	10.1

World Record — 31 pounds, caught in Cowichan Bay, British Columbia, in 1947. A 39-pound, 2-ounce coho was taken by state fisheries workers in the Manistee River, Michigan, in 1973.

Chum Salmon (Oncorhynchus keta)

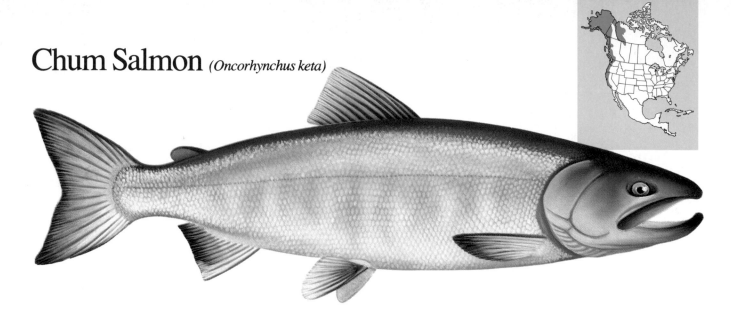

Common Names — Dog salmon, calico salmon, autumn salmon.

Description — Silvery sides, often with faint vertical bands. Like sockeyes, they lack distinct dark spots. But the pupil is wider in comparison to the total width of the eye than that of a sockeye. The chum has less than 30 short, stubby gill rakers (photo at right); the sockeye 30 or more long, fine gill rakers.

Hybrids — Known to hybridize with pink salmon.

Table Quality — The flesh is pinkish to yellowish and has a lower fat content than the reddish flesh of coho, chinook or sockeye salmon. The eating quality is good, but considered inferior to that of other salmon.

Sporting Qualities — Chum salmon are strong fighters, but do not provide much of a sport fishery. Because they enter the streams in an advanced state of sexual maturity, they spend no more than 2 or 3 weeks in fresh water. Some are caught in tidal areas of coastal streams. The best lures are spinners and small spoons.

Habitat — Anadromous, entering Pacific coastal streams to spawn. They are not strong leapers, so they swim upstream only to the first major barrier, which generally is not far. They prefer water temperatures from 54° to 57°F, and avoid temperatures above 59°.

Food Habits — At sea, chum salmon feed on plankton, small fish, squid, crab larvae and crustaceans. They do not feed after they enter the streams, but can still be caught on artificial lures.

Spawning Habits — In some rivers, there is one run of chum salmon in summer and another in fall, but in most cases the only run is in fall. This accounts for the name "autumn salmon," also applied to pink salmon. Summer-run fish are generally smaller and do not swim as far upstream.

A female digs one or more redds in gravel riffles. Spawning begins at water temperatures from 45° to 55°F. After spawning, the female guards the nest for a few days, then dies.

SPAWNING MALE CHUM — Hooked upper jaw, noticeable kype, large canine teeth, and a slight hump ahead of the dorsal fin. Sides olive to grayish, with purplish vertical bands. Tips of anal and pelvic fins are often white. Spawning females have similar coloration.

Age and Growth — Chum salmon generally spawn at age 2 to 7, most commonly at age 4. Both sexes die after spawning. The average adult weighs 5 to 10 pounds; males are generally heavier than females.

Typical Length (inches) at Various Ages

Age	1	2	3	4	5
Length	8.4	17.3	24.2	29.9	33.7

Typical Weight (pounds) at Various Lengths (inches)

Length	15	18	21	24	27	30	33
Weight	1.8	2.8	4.3	6.1	8.9	12.5	16.9

World Record — 32 pounds, caught in Behm Canal, Alaska, in 1985. Chum salmon up to 45 pounds have been taken by commercial fishermen.

Spawning female chum salmon — King Salmon Creek, Alaska

Sockeye Salmon *(Oncorhynchus nerka)*

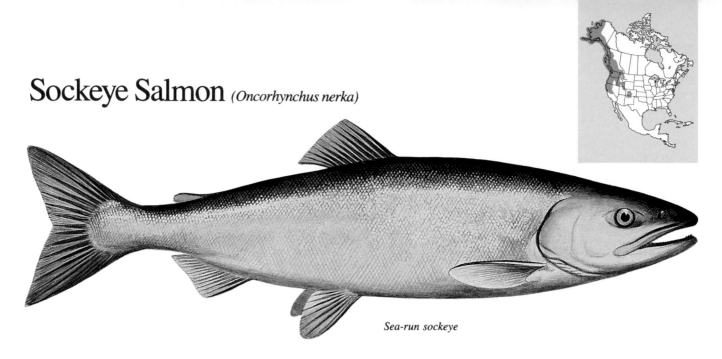

Sea-run sockeye

Common Names — Red salmon, blueback salmon. Landlocked form is called kokanee, koke, redfish and silver trout.

Description — Silvery sides with brilliant steel-blue to bluish green back. No distinct black spots, but may have black speckles on back. Outward appearance similar to that of chum salmon, but they have 30 or more long, slender gill rakers on the first gill arch (photo at right); chums have less than 30 short, stubby gill rakers. The pupil of a sockeye is smaller in relation to the rest of the eye than that of a chum.

Forms — The kokanee is a dwarf landlocked form of the sockeye.

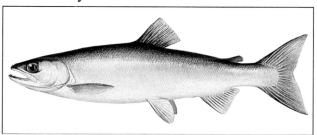

KOKANEE — The coloration is identical to that of a sea-run sockeye, although the body is often slimmer because of the smaller size. Spawning kokanee undergo the same color changes as spawning sea-run sockeyes.

Table Quality — Excellent; the meat is oily, bright red and very flavorful. Considered one of the best eating of the Pacific salmon.

Sporting Qualities — Sockeyes are strong fighters and good leapers, but until recently were not widely sought by anglers because their plankton-eating habits made them difficult to catch. However, fishermen have discovered that sockeyes can be caught on small baits and lures like a tiny hook baited with a salmon egg or piece of worm, or a fly. Cowbells work well as an attractor. Kokanee can be caught during the open-water season, but are more easily caught through the ice.

Habitat — Anadromous, usually spawning in streams that have lakes as their source. Kokanee thrive in large, oligotrophic lakes in the West. They are *pelagic*, meaning that they roam the open waters of a lake to find food. Sockeyes prefer water temperatures of 50° to 55°F.

Food Habits — The diet of sea-run sockeyes consists mainly of plankton and small crustaceans,

rarely fish. Kokanee also eat plankton, but sometimes feed on small bottom organisms.

Spawning Habits — Sockeyes run upstream to just below a lake outlet. Some spawn in the lake itself or in inlet streams. Spawning begins in late summer or early fall, at water temperatures from 45° to 52°F, and lasts only a few days. Females dig a series of redds; both sexes guard the nest until death. Kokanee spawn in fall, usually in outlet streams.

SPAWNING MALE SOCKEYE — Sides brilliant red, head dull green, and lower jaw white. Long, strongly hooked upper jaw; well-developed kype; small canine teeth; and a prominent hump ahead of the dorsal fin.

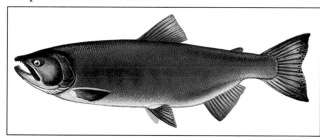

SPAWNING FEMALE SOCKEYE — The body does not change shape, but the head turns dull green and the sides red. The amount of reddish coloration varies in different populations, but is usually less intense than that of the male.

Age and Growth — Most sockeyes spawn at age 4, but some spawn as early as age 3 or as late as age 8. Males weigh more than females of the same age.

Typical Length (inches) at Various Ages

Age	1	2	3	4	5
Sea-run	3.5	4.7	22.2	24.9	26.4
Kokanee	4.3	9.8	12.1	15.1	18.4

Typical Weight (pounds) at Various Lengths (inches)

Length	12	14	16	18	20	22	24	26	28
Weight	0.7	1.0	1.4	2.1	2.8	3.8	4.9	6.3	7.8

World Record — Sea-run: 12 pounds, 8 ounces, caught in the Situk River, Alaska, in 1983. Alaska lists a 16-pounder, caught in the Kenai River in 1974. Kokanee: 6 pounds, 9 ounces, caught in Priest Lake, Idaho, in 1975.

Golden Trout *(Salmo aguabonita)*

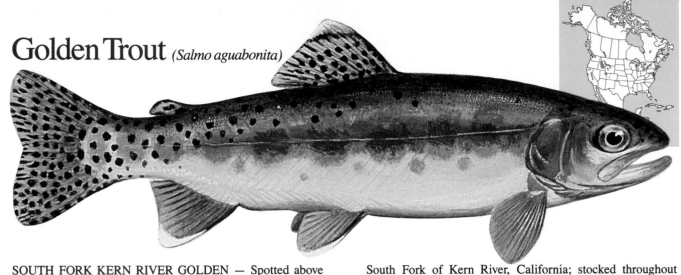

SOUTH FORK KERN RIVER GOLDEN — Spotted above lateral line; a few spots below lateral line near tail. Native to South Fork of Kern River, California; stocked throughout golden trout range.

Common Names — Kern River trout and mountain trout.

Description — Generally considered the most beautiful of all trout. The sides are brilliant gold and have a crimson band which runs through about 10 dark, oval *parr* marks. The parr marks persist through life. The tail is spotted, and the dorsal, pelvic and anal fins have white tips. When golden trout are stocked at low altitudes, they lack the brilliant colors. See subspecies descriptons.

Subspecies — Experts disagree in the taxonomy of golden trout, but most recognize two subspecies, the South Fork Kern River golden *(Salmo agua-bonita aguabonita)*, and the Little Kern River golden *(Salmo aguabonita whitei)*.

LITTLE KERN RIVER GOLDEN — Spotted above and below lateral line. Native to Little Kern River, California; not widely stocked.

Hybrids — Often hybridizes with rainbow and occasionally with cutthroat.

Table Quality — The pinkish flesh is slightly oilier than that of most other trout, but is excellent when eaten fresh or smoked. It does not keep well for extended periods.

Sporting Qualities — The mystique surrounding golden trout makes them highly desired gamefish. They are most common in mountainous areas accessible only by hiking. Good fighters for their size, goldens can be very fussy, taking only flies that closely match the insects they are eating. They can also be caught on tiny spinners and spoons, and on natural baits such as worms, crustaceans, insects and salmon eggs.

Habitat — Originally, golden trout were found only in cold mountain lakes and streams above an elevation of 6,000 feet. But they have been stocked in many small lakes at lower elevations. They can tolerate temperatures up to 72°F, but most of their waters do not get that warm. They prefer water of about 58° to 62°.

Food Habits — The diet consists mainly of small crustaceans and adult and immature insects, especially caddisflies and midges.

Spawning Habits — Golden trout spawn in early to mid-summer, usually at a water temperature of about 50°F. Stream-dwelling fish spawn in the stream itself or in small tributaries. Lake dwellers spawn in inlets or outlets. The female digs several redds, usually at the tail of a pool, and deposits eggs in each. After spawning, the adults return to their home pools or to the lake.

SPAWNING MALE GOLDEN (South Fork subspecies) — Reddish orange color on cheeks, belly and lateral line becomes more intense, as does gold color on flanks and white on fins. Jaws somewhat longer than those of a normal male.

Age and Growth — Golden trout grow slowly. In most waters, the maximum life span is 7 years, with the fish topping off at less than 1 pound.

Typical Length (inches) at Various Ages

Age	1	2	3	4	5	6
Length	3.8	5.7	8.6	10.2	11.6	14.0

Typical Weight (pounds) at Various Lengths (inches)

Length	6	8	10	12	14	16	18
Weight	.09	.21	.39	.70	1.1	1.6	2.2

World Record — 11 pounds, caught in Cook's Lake, Wyoming, in 1948.

12-inch South Fork golden — Alger Lake, California

YELLOWSTONE CUTTHROAT — Spots above and below lateral line, more heavily concentrated toward the rear.

Largest spots no larger than pupil of eye. Found mainly in lakes and streams in Montana, Wyoming, Idaho and Utah.

18-inch West Slope cutthroat — Howe Lake, Glacier National Park, Montana

Cutthroat Trout *(Salmo clarki)*

Common Names — Native trout, cut, red throat, mountain trout, black-spotted trout.

Description — Easily identified by red or orange slash marks on throat, although these may be faint in sea-run fish. Cutthroat have a patch of teeth at the base of the tongue; rainbows do not. See descriptions of each subspecies.

Subspecies — Some authorities recognize as many as fourteen subspecies of cutthroat, but only five are of major importance to fishermen. They include: Yellowstone cutthroat *(Salmo clarki bouvieri),* coastal cutthroat or harvest trout *(Salmo clarki clarki),* West Slope cutthroat *(Salmo clarki lewisi),* Lahontan

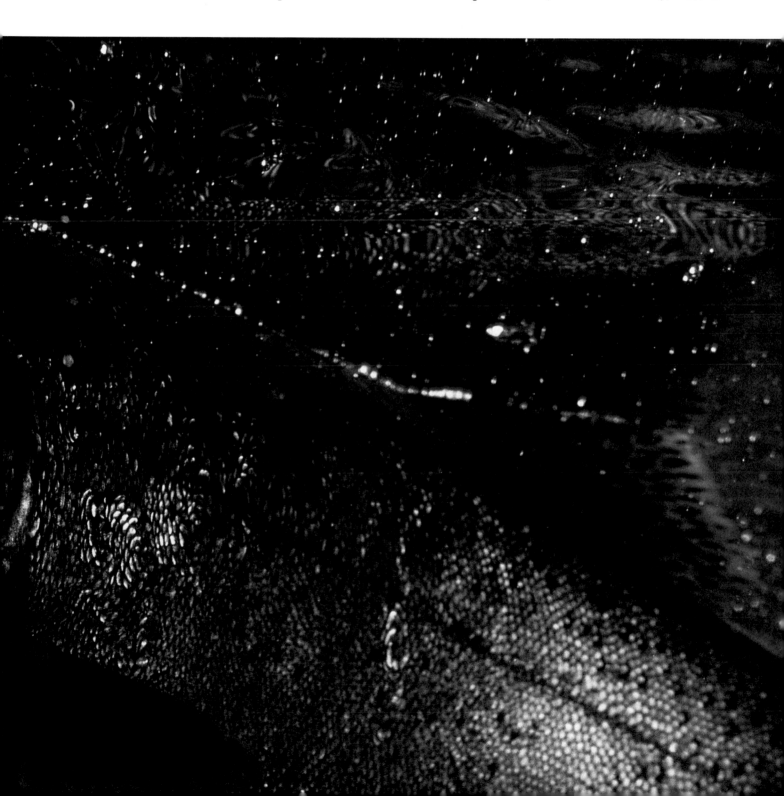

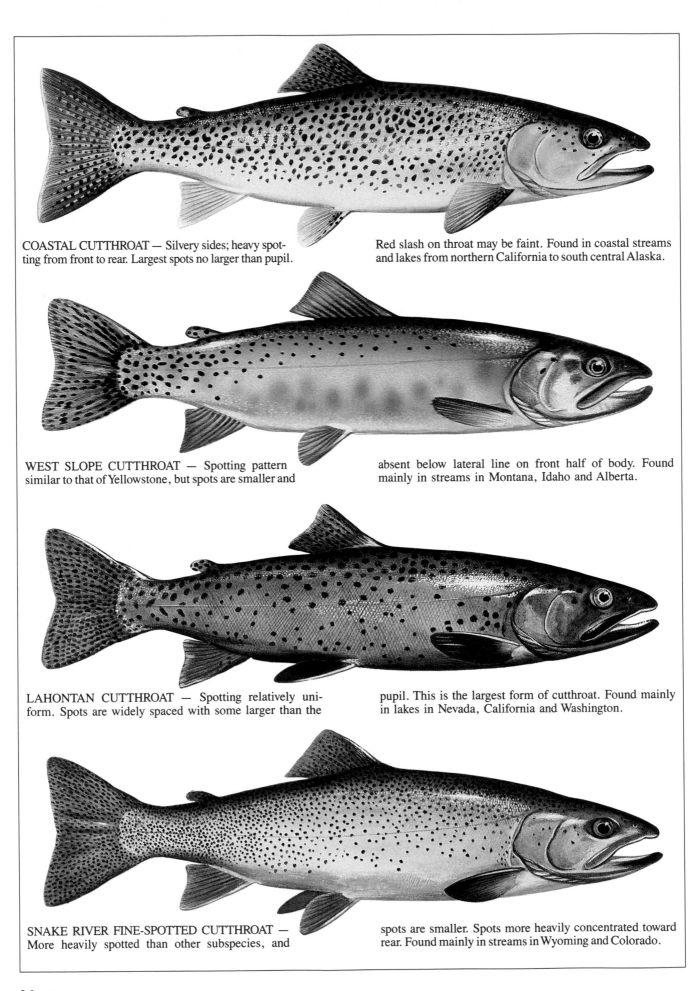

COASTAL CUTTHROAT — Silvery sides; heavy spotting from front to rear. Largest spots no larger than pupil. Red slash on throat may be faint. Found in coastal streams and lakes from northern California to south central Alaska.

WEST SLOPE CUTTHROAT — Spotting pattern similar to that of Yellowstone, but spots are smaller and absent below lateral line on front half of body. Found mainly in streams in Montana, Idaho and Alberta.

LAHONTAN CUTTHROAT — Spotting relatively uniform. Spots are widely spaced with some larger than the pupil. This is the largest form of cutthroat. Found mainly in lakes in Nevada, California and Washington.

SNAKE RIVER FINE-SPOTTED CUTTHROAT — More heavily spotted than other subspecies, and spots are smaller. Spots more heavily concentrated toward rear. Found mainly in streams in Wyoming and Colorado.

GREENBACK CUTTHROAT have larger spots than other subspecies. They are native to Colorado, but their populations declined to the point where they were considered "endangered." Recently, however, the fish have been stocked in several Colorado streams and populations have recovered enough to change their classification to "threatened."

cutthroat *(Salmo clarki henshawi)*, and Snake River fine-spotted cutthroat (no official subspecies name).

Other subspecies include: Bonneville cutthroat, Colorado River cutthroat, Greenback cutthroat, Rio Grande cutthroat, Paiute cutthroat, yellowfin cutthroat, mountain cutthroat, Humbolt cutthroat, and Alvord cutthroat.

Hybrids — Cutthroat hybridize with rainbow to produce the cutbow, and they sometimes hybridize with golden trout.

Table Quality — Excellent. Flesh varies from white to red.

Sporting Qualities — The favorite of many western anglers, cutthroat are easy to catch compared to most other trout species. They are strong fighters, but not as acrobatic as rainbows. They can be caught on wet flies, dry flies, nymphs, and streamers, and are not as selective as rainbows or browns. Spoons, spinners and earthworms also work well.

Habitat — Found in coldwater streams and mountain lakes in the West. The coastal cutthroat spends most of its life at sea, entering Pacific Coast streams to spawn. Unlike other seagoing trout, the coastal cutthroat never ventures far from the stream mouths. Cutthroat prefer water temperatures from 55° to 62°F.

Food Habits — Eat mostly insects and small fish; occasionally feed on trout eggs, crustaceans, frogs and earthworms.

Spawning Habits — Cutthroat spawn in spring, building their redds in gravel beds in small streams.

They do not guard the eggs or fry. Individual fish usually spawn only in alternate years. Cutthroat do not spawn successfully in lakes.

SPAWNING MALE (Yellowstone) — Yellowish green on back, red on side of head, and yellow on flanks becomes more intense. No noticeable kype.

Age and Growth — Maximum age about 9 years; more commonly 4 to 7 years. Growth varies greatly among different subspecies. West Slopes grow most slowly; Lahontans most rapidly. Males generally grow fastest and attain the largest size. In most waters, cutthroat rarely exceed 5 pounds.

Typical Length (inches) at Various Ages

Age	1	2	3	4	5	6	7
Coastal	4.2	5.2	13.4	13.8	14.3	15.1	16.3
West Slope	4.1	5.8	8.0	11.0	13.0	14.8	—
Yellowstone	2.1	5.5	9.2	12.5	15.8	19.7	—
Lahontan	9.1	12.3	15.3	18.2	20.6	23.7	25.5
Snake River	7.8	10.5	14.0	17.9	19.1	—	—

Typical Weight (pounds) at Various Lengths (inches)

Length	10	11	12	13	14	16	18	20	22
Weight	.43	.57	.72	.93	1.2	1.7	2.4	3.3	4.7

World Record — 41 pounds, caught in Pyramid Lake, Nevada, in 1925. This fish was a Lahontan cutthroat.

COMMON RAINBOW — Pinkish stripe on sides and pink patch on gill cover. Dark spots on back and sides, above and below lateral line; usually has some spots on gill cover. Widely stocked in lakes and streams throughout most of North America.

8-pound rainbow (common subspecies) — Naknek River, Alaska

Rainbow Trout *(Salmo gairdneri)*

Common Names — Bow, red-band trout, silver trout, redsides. Dozens of other names are given to varieties based on their origin. For example, the Eagle Lake rainbow originated in Eagle Lake, California.

Description — Silvery sides with a horizontal red band that varies in intensity in different populations. The back is bluish to greenish. The tail has radiating rows of black spots. Unlike cutthroats, rainbows have no teeth on the tongue. See description of each subspecies.

Subspecies — There are more than a hundred varieties of rainbow, but only three sub-

species: the common rainbow *(Salmo gairdneri gairdneri)*, coastal rainbow or steelhead *(Salmo gairdneri irideus)*, and Kamloops rainbow *(Salmo gairdneri kamloops)*.

KAMLOOPS RAINBOW — Coloration and spotting similar to those of common rainbow, but the body is much deeper. Native to Kamloops Lake, British Columbia, but widely stocked in the northern U.S. and Canada.

COASTAL RAINBOW (STEELHEAD) — Long, sleek, silvery body with a faint pink stripe or no stripe. The gill cover may have a pinkish patch, but with few or no black spots. Few spots below the lateral line. Found along the Pacific coast from California to Alaska. Also stocked in large inland lakes, particularly the Great Lakes.

Hybrids — Commonly hybridizes with cutthroat to produce the cutbow, and with golden trout.

Table Quality — The flesh ranges from bright red to white, depending on the fish's diet, and is considered excellent eating either fresh or smoked. Whole rainbows of ¾ to 1 pound are often featured in gourmet restaurants.

Sporting Qualities — The leaping ability of the rainbow is legendary. A hooked rainbow almost always skyrockets from the water, often a half-dozen times, before coming to the net. Rainbows are less wary than brown trout and more willing to bite. They are a favorite of fly fishermen, but can also be caught on spinners, spoons, plugs, and a wide variety of baits ranging from worms to small marshmallows.

Habitat — Nonmigratory rainbows prefer cool, clear streams and lakes, but can survive in warm-water lakes, as long as there is cool, oxygenated water in the depths. Steelhead roam widely at sea or in large inland lakes. A steelhead tagged in the Aleutian Islands was caught six months later in a Washington river 2,400 miles from the tagging site. Rainbows prefer water from 55° to 60°F, but will tolerate temperatures up to 75°.

19-inch rainbow about to take stonefly nymph — Middle Fork, Flathead River, Montana

Food Habits — The diet consists mainly of immature and adult insects, plankton, crustaceans, fish eggs, and small fish. But rainbows consume far fewer fish than brown trout. Their habit of taking adult insects on the surface makes dry-fly fishing particularly effective.

Spawning Habits — Most varieties of rainbow are spring spawners, but one variety or another will be spawning every month of the year. Spawning takes place in a small tributary of a larger stream, or in an inlet or outlet of a lake, normally at water temperatures of 50° to 60°F.

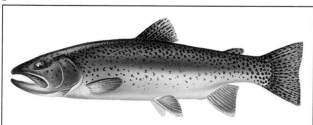

SPAWNING MALE (common subspecies) — Sides duskier than normal rainbow, and reddish lateral band more intense. Lower jaw has a pronounced kype.

Steelhead normally spawn in large, swift, boulder-strewn streams. The spawning site is usually the gravelly tail of a pool, or the riffle at the head of a pool. The female digs several redds and deposits eggs in each. After spawning, the adults return to their home stream or lake. Steelhead may enter the streams several months before spawning and stay several months after spawning has been completed.

Age and Growth — Growth is highly variable, depending on the habitat. A typical stream-dwelling rainbow grows to about 1 pound in four years. But in a large lake where food is plentiful, a rainbow could reach 15 pounds in the same amount of time. Rainbows may live up to 11 years, but the usual life span is 4 to 6 years.

Typical Length (inches) at Various Ages

Age	1	2	3	4	5	6	7
Common	3.2	7.9	11.1	13.5	15.9	16.6	18.5
Coastal	—	—	22.5	27.7	30.4	32.7	33.6
Kamloops	4.2	11.4	15.9	20.8	26.1	—	—

Typical Weight (pounds) at Various Lengths (inches)

Length	9	12	15	18	21	24	27
Weight	.36	.68	1.3	2.3	3.6	5.4	8.4

World Record — Landlocked rainbow: 27 pounds, 3 ounces, caught in the Ganaraska River, Ontario, in 1984. A 52-pounder was once netted in Jewel Lake, British Columbia. Steelhead: 42 pounds, 2 ounces, caught at Bell Island, Alaska, in 1970.

Brown Trout *(Salmo trutta)*

Common Names — German brown, Loch Leven trout and brownie. Sea-run browns are often called sea trout.

Description — Sides have a light brown or yellow cast with black spots and usually some orange or red spots. The spots often have whitish to bluish halos. The tail generally lacks spots, but may have a few.

Subspecies — Brown trout were originally introduced from Germany and Scotland, and subspecies designations given to stocks from each country. But because of widespread stocking and genetic mixing, these subspecies are no longer recognized. Sea-run browns are not considered a subspecies.

SEA-RUN BROWN — Pale yellow to silvery sides, often with X- or Y-shaped marks similar to those of sea-run Atlantic salmon. The adipose fin of a brown is spotted; that of an Atlantic is not. Found in rivers along the East and West coasts, and in large, deep inland lakes.

Hybrids — Brown trout hybridize with brook trout to produce the tiger trout.

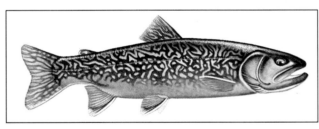

TIGER TROUT — Sides are usually greenish to brownish with distinct light, wormlike markings. Lower fins may have whitish leading edges. Much less wary than brown trout.

Table Quality — The meat usually has a pinkish or yellowish hue and a good flavor. But it is not considered as good as that of brook trout.

Sporting Qualities — A strong fighter, but not as acrobatic as a rainbow. It is the wariest of all trout; big ones may feed only at night. Browns can be taken with a variety of dry flies, nymphs and streamers. They will also strike spoons, spinners and plugs. But many of the biggest ones are caught on live bait, especially nightcrawlers and large minnows.

Habitat — Browns can live in warmer, more turbid water than other trout. They prefer water from 60° to 65°F, but can survive at 75° and will tolerate 80° for short periods. They thrive in coolwater streams and lakes, but cannot reproduce in lakes.

Food Habits — Primarily fish eaters, brown trout also consume crayfish and terrestrial and aquatic insects. Large browns prey on smaller trout and other gamefish.

4-pound brown trout — Rush River, Wisconsin

Spawning Habits — Spawn in fall, usually at water temperatures of 44° to 48°F. They move into shallow, gravelly areas of their home stream or into gravelly tributaries. Females dig a redd, and after spawning, cover it with gravel and abandon it.

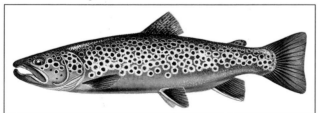

SPAWNING MALE BROWN — The typical yellowish coloration becomes more intense, often taking on an orange hue. The lower jaw develops a strong kype and the lower fins often become slate-colored.

Age and Growth — Brown trout grow rapidly, but are not particularly long-lived. Few survive beyond age 8. Lake-dwelling browns grow much faster than stream browns; males faster than females.

Typical Length (inches) at Various Ages

Age	1	2	3	4	5	6
Lake	6.7	12.3	16.6	19.3	22.2	25.4
Stream	6.4	9.3	12.5	14.4	16.6	18.0

Typical Weight (pounds) at Various Lengths (inches)

Length	12	15	18	21	24	27	30
Weight	.70	1.4	2.4	4.0	6.2	9.0	12.5

World Record — 35 pounds, 15 ounces, caught in Lake Nahuel Huapi, Argentina, in 1952.

Atlantic Salmon *(Salmo salar)*

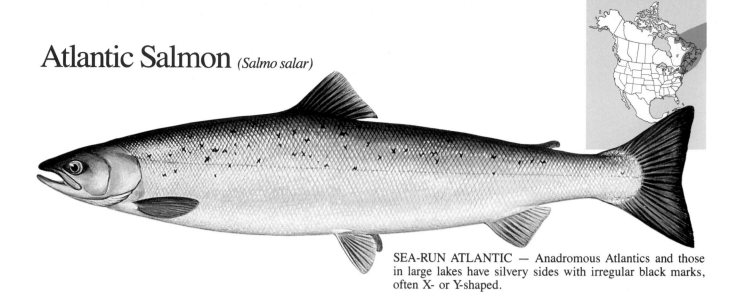

SEA-RUN ATLANTIC — Anadromous Atlantics and those in large lakes have silvery sides with irregular black marks, often X- or Y-shaped.

Common Names — The landlocked form is called landlocked salmon, Ouananiche, or Sebago salmon.

Description — Silvery to yellowish brown sides with dark spots. Atlantics may resemble brown trout, but the tail is slightly forked rather than square, and there are no spots on the adipose fin.

Forms — Two distinct forms: sea-run and landlocked (see descriptions of each).

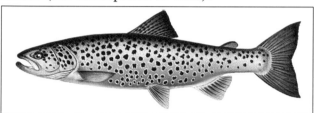

LANDLOCKED ATLANTIC (Ouananiche strain) — Sides have brownish to bluish cast; spots larger than those of sea-run Atlantic and often have light halos. The Ouananiche is the most heavily spotted form of landlocked salmon.

Table Quality — Excellent, although sea-run Atlantics are so rare and so valuable as sport fish that they always should be returned to the water. Landlocked salmon are plentiful enough in some areas to allow harvest for food.

Sporting Qualities — Atlantic salmon are among the most acrobatic of all gamefish. They make long, powerful runs which can quickly empty a reel. They rise well to a dry fly, and many consider fly fishing the only sporting method of taking these magnificent fish.

Habitat — Anadromous form spawns in clear, coldwater streams along the North Atlantic Coast, especially in Canada. Landlocked form inhabits clear, coldwater lakes, with gravelly inlet streams for spawning. Atlantic salmon prefer water from 53° to 59°F.

Food Habits — Atlantics eat mainly crustaceans, insects and small fish. They do not feed after they enter the streams; their willingness to take a fly is considered a reflex.

Spawning Habits — Spawn in fall, often swimming far upstream and negotiating seemingly impassable falls. The female digs a very large redd in a gravel riffle. Spawning takes place at water temperatures from 42° to 50°F. The female abandons the nest after spawning, and if she survives, usually returns to the sea. The male often winters in the river. Some Atlantics live to spawn two or three times. Landlocked salmon spawn in tributaries of the lakes where they live.

SPAWNING MALE ATLANTIC — Sides turn yellowish to brownish and may develop some orange spots. Well-developed kype on lower jaw.

Age and Growth — Atlantics spend 2 to 3 years in their home stream, and up to 6 more years at sea or in a lake. Male Atlantics grow faster than females; sea-runs faster than landlocks.

Typical Length (inches) at Various Ages

Age	1	2	3	4	5	6
Sea-run	(stream life)	21.9	30.2	35.0	39.1
Landlocked	5.2	14.9	17.9	19.3	20.3	23.4

Typical Weight (pounds) at Various Lengths (inches)

Length	15	18	21	24	27	30	33	36	39
Weight	1.3	2.3	3.9	5.2	6.6	9.8	14.5	19.4	24.5

World Record — Sea-run: 79 pounds, 2 ounces, caught in the Tana River, Norway, in 1928. Sea-run Atlantics over 100 pounds have been taken by commercial fishermen. Landlocked: 22 pounds, 8 ounces, caught in Sebago Lake, Maine, in 1907.

Sea-run Atlantic salmon — St. Mary's River, Nova Scotia

Lake Trout *(Salvelinus namaycush)*

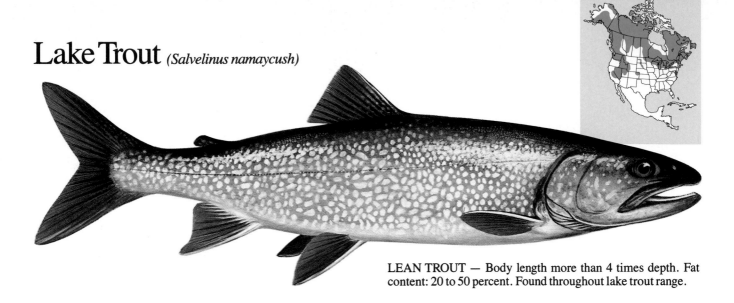

LEAN TROUT — Body length more than 4 times depth. Fat content: 20 to 50 percent. Found throughout lake trout range.

Common Names — Laker, mackinaw, gray trout, togue.

Description — Deeply forked tail; light spots on a background varying from light green or gray, to dark green, brown or black; light spots cover the head. See subspecies descriptions.

Subspecies — Although there are dozens of geographic races of lake trout, most experts recognize only two subspecies: the lean trout *(Salvelinus namaycush namaycush)*, and the siscowet or fat trout *(Salvelinus namaycush siscowet)*. The fat trout is named for its high fat content.

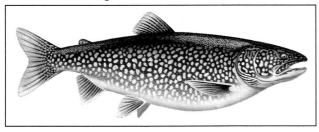

SISCOWET — Body length less than 4 times depth; color lighter than lean trout and spots slightly smaller. Fat content 70 to 90 percent. Found only in Lake Superior.

Hybrids — Lake trout occasionally hybridize with Arctic char. Female lake trout are artificially crossed with male brook trout to produce splake or wendigo, which are stocked in numerous oligotrophic lakes in the northern states and Canada.

SPLAKE — Back has light, wormlike markings; sides have light spots. Tail not as deeply forked as that of a lake trout; tips of tail rounder.

Table Quality — Excellent when eaten fresh or smoked. But the high fat content causes the flesh to turn rancid when frozen for long periods. Depending on the fish's diet, the meat can vary from bright orange to off-white.

Sporting Qualities — Lake trout do not leap, but instead wage a strong, determined underwater battle. Most are taken by trolling with spoons or minnowlike plugs attached to wire-line rigs or downriggers. They can also be taken by bottom-fishing with whole or cut fish. Siscowets are seldom caught on hook and line because they live at extreme depths.

Habitat — Lake trout require, cold, clear, well-oxygenated water, so they are found almost exclusively in oligotrophic lakes. In summer they often move to depths of 50 to 100 feet, but in spring and fall you can find them at depths of 20 feet or less. They prefer water from 48° to 52°F. Siscowets usually live at depths of 300 to 500 feet, but have been found as deep as 600 feet.

Food Habits — In most waters, lake trout rely heavily on small fish like ciscoes, smelt or sculpins. But in some lakes, they feed almost exclusively on plankton, insects or crustaceans. In this situation, lake trout never reach the size of those in fish-eating populations.

Spawning Habits — Spawn in fall at water temperatures of 48° to 55°F, usually on rocky reefs less than 40 feet deep and sometimes on reefs only a foot deep. Occasionally, lake trout swim up rivers to spawn. They do not build a redd, but scatter the eggs over rocks. The eggs slip into crevices where they can incubate over the winter, safe from predators. After spawning, the adults disperse, sometimes moving as far as 100 miles from the spawning reef. A lake trout usually spawns on the same reef each year.

8- to 10-pound lake trout — White Otter Lake, Ontario

Age and Growth — Lake trout are slow-growing and long-lived, sometimes reaching an age of 40 years. In the far North, it may take 15 years for a laker to reach 2 pounds.

Typical Length (inches) at Various Ages

Age	1	3	5	7	9	11	13	15
Length	4.0	9.3	13.2	16.7	20.2	24.0	30.1	34.5

Typical Weight (pounds) at Various Lengths (inches)

Length	15	20	25	30	35	40	45	50
Lean trout	1.2	2.7	5.6	11.9	17.0	27.7	37.5	47.9
Siscowet	1.2	3.3	7.0	13.0	21.8	34.3	—	—

World Record — 65 pounds, caught in Great Bear Lake, Northwest Territories, in 1970. A 102-pound lake trout was taken in a gillnet in Lake Athabasca, Saskatchewan, in 1961.

16-inch brook trout — Brule River, Wisconsin

Brook Trout *(Salvelinus fontinalis)*

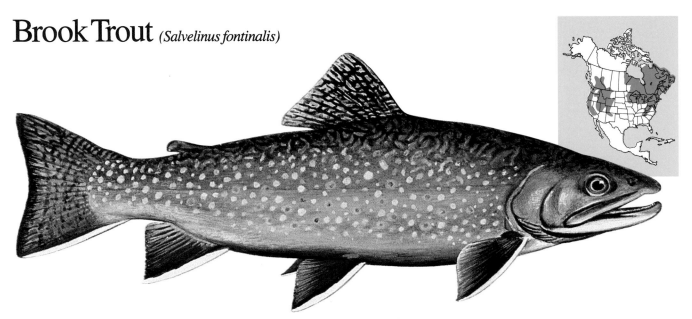

Common Names — Eastern brook trout, brookie, speckled trout, native trout and squaretail. A sea-run brook trout is called a salter or sea trout; a brook trout in the Great Lakes that migrates up tributaries to spawn is known as a coaster.

Description — Brownish to greenish back with pale wormlike marks; sides with pale spots and some small red spots with blue halos; tail almost square. Lower fins have white leading edges. Sea-run brookies and coasters are more silvery and the spots less intense.

Habitat — Brook trout thrive in streams, lakes, and ponds that are cold and clear. They prefer water of 52° to 56°F. Because of their coldwater habits, brook trout often are confined to the headwaters of spring-fed streams. Although there is still plenty of good brook trout water in the United States, a great deal of prime habitat has been lost to stream channelization, dam building, pollution, and streambank erosion caused by deforestation and overgrazing. Today, the best brook trout waters are in sparsely populated regions of Labrador, Quebec and Manitoba.

Food Habits — The diet is extremely varied, depending on what is available. Some of the food items found in brook trout stomachs include tiny larval insects, small fish, field mice and even snakes.

Spawning Habits — Brook trout spawn in late summer or fall at water temperatures of 40° to 49°F. The usual spawning site is a gravel bed in the headwaters of a small stream. Sea-run brook trout move into their home streams in spring and early summer, but do not spawn until fall. The female digs several redds, depositing eggs in each. The parents make no attempt to guard the nests. Unlike most stream-dwelling trout and char, brook trout can also spawn successfully in lakes, assuming there is enough upwelling from springs to keep the eggs aerated.

SPAWNING MALE BROOK TROUT — Lower jaw develops strong kype. All colors intensify with flanks and belly turning orange-red; some black pigmentation on either side of belly.

Age and Growth — Slow-growing compared to most other trout and char, brook trout tend to overpopulate their habitat and become stunted. Surprisingly, the fastest growth occurs in the northern part of their range. In most populations, males grow slightly faster than females, but do not live as long. Maximum age is about 15 years.

Typical Length (inches) at Various Ages

Age	1	2	3	4	5	6	7
North	7.1	8.7	10.2	11.7	13.1	16.4	18.0
South	5.4	6.7	7.8	9.2	9.7	11.2	—

Typical Weight (pounds) at Various Lengths (inches)

Length	6	8	10	12	14	16	18
Weight	.09	.23	.47	.83	1.4	2.0	2.8

World Record — 14 pounds, 8 ounces, caught in the Nipigon River, Ontario, in 1916. Senator Daniel Webster is said to have caught a salter of the same size in the Carmans River, New York, in 1827.

Forms — There are two ecologically different forms: a short-lived, slow-growing form common to many small streams and lakes throughout the range; and a longer-lived, faster-growing form found in lakes, rivers and estuaries in the northern part of the range.

Hybrids — Male brook trout can be crossed with female lake trout to produce splake (page 46). Brook trout also hybridize with brown trout to produce tiger trout (page 42), and occasionally with bull trout and Arctic char.

Table Quality — A superb table fish, considered better eating than brown or rainbow trout. Depending on the fish's diet, the flesh can vary from white to bright orange.

Sporting Qualities — Brook trout are not spectacular leapers, but are powerful fighters for their size. They will take a dry fly, but subsurface flies generally work better. Many are caught on small spoons and spinners, and on worms, leeches, minnows and a variety of other live baits. Brookies are one of the least wary and easiest to catch of the salmonids.

Bull Trout *(Salvelinus confluentus)*

Common Names — Until recently, bull trout were considered the same species as Dolly Varden. Most anglers have difficulty telling them apart, so the two go by the same common names which include red-spotted char, salmon-trout, bull char and Dolly.

Description — Grayish to dark green sides, with whitish to pinkish spots; white leading edges on lower fins; head longer, broader and more flattened than that of a Dolly Varden.

Hybrids — Bull trout hybridize with Dolly Varden and brook trout.

Table Quality — The flesh is normally pink and has a good flavor, but is not as highly regarded as that of brook trout or Arctic char.

Sporting Qualities — Bull trout have a reputation as predators on other, more highly valued salmonids. Although bull trout are good fighters, they have not gained much popularity with anglers. They are difficult to catch on flies; most are taken by trolling in deep water with spoons or plugs on downriggers or wire-line rigs.

Habitat — Primarily oligotrophic lakes and deep pools of large, coldwater streams. They prefer water temperatures from 45° to 55°F, and are usually found close to bottom. Except in Alaska, bull trout are not anadromous.

Food Habits — The majority of the diet consists of fish, but bull trout also eat crustaceans, molluscs and insects.

Spawning Habits — Bull trout spawn in late summer or fall, normally at water temperatures of 45° to 50°F. Lake dwellers swim up inlet streams; stream dwellers move upstream to small tributaries. The female digs a redd in a gravel riffle. After spawning, the fish return to the lake or to deep holes in the home stream.

SPAWNING MALE BULL TROUT — Overall coloration intensifies; lower jaw develops kype. Flanks and belly become yellowish orange.

Age and Growth — Growth is slow for the first 3 to 4 years, but then accelerates rapidly. Bull trout may live as long as 19 years.

Typical Length (inches) at Various Ages

Age	1	2	3	4	5	6	7	8
Length	2.8	5.1	7.7	12.3	17.3	22.2	25.4	27.9

Typical Weight (pounds) at Various Lengths (inches)

Length	16	19	22	25	28	31	34	37
Weight	1.4	2.1	3.5	5.5	8.7	12.9	19.1	25.0

World Record — 32 pounds, caught in Lake Pend Oreille, Idaho, in 1949. Until recently, this fish was considered a Dolly Varden.

6-pound bull trout — Flathead Lake, Montana

Dolly Varden *(Salvelinus malma)*

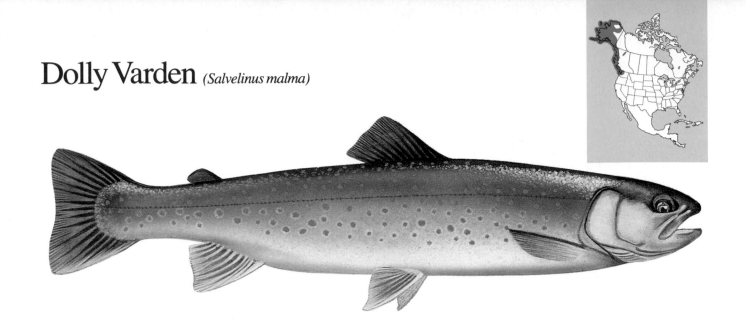

Common Names — Dolly, red-spotted char, bull char, salmon-trout. Until recently, Dolly Varden and bull trout were considered the same species. The fish gets its name from Miss Dolly Varden, a Dickens character who wore a green calico dress with pink polka dots.

Description — Silvery green sides with reddish to pinkish spots, and white leading edges on the lower fins. Closely resembles Arctic char and bull trout. Dollies normally have smaller spots than char, although the size of the spots varies considerably. The largest spots are usually smaller than the pupil. The head of a Dolly is shorter, narrower and less flattened than that of a bull trout. Sea-run Dollies resemble landlocks, but the sides are more silvery, and the color of the spots less intense.

Subspecies — Currently, only one subspecies is recognized in North America, the northern Dolly Varden *(Salvelinus malma malma)*. There is another subspecies in the Far East. Some biologists believe that Dollies found south of the Alaska peninsula should be given subspecies status. These fish grow to only about 5 pounds, but those farther north reach 12 pounds.

Hybrids — Dollies are known to hybridize with bull trout.

Table Quality — Good; the meat is pink and flavorful.

Sporting Qualities — Easy to catch and capable of waging a good fight on light tackle. They make strong runs, but seldom leap. Small ones eagerly take dry flies; larger ones prefer streamers, spinners, spoons or plugs fished near bottom. Dollies also bite well on natural bait, especially salmon eggs and minnows.

Habitat — Most Dolly Varden are anadromous coastal fish; bull trout are found mainly in large, coldwater lakes and streams in mountainous areas. After going to sea, Dollies periodically stray back to coastal streams which are not necessarily their home streams. No other salmonid shows this random straying behavior. Landlocked Dollies are found in many western lakes and streams. Dollies prefer water temperatures of 50° to 55°F.

Food Habits — Dolly Varden have a reputation for consuming large numbers of young salmon. While it is true they eat some, they are no more a threat than rainbows, cutthroats or immature coho salmon. Dollies also eat other small fish, the remains of dead fish, salmon eggs that have drifted from the redd, and many types of larval and adult insects.

Spawning Habits — At age 5 or 6, sea-run Dollies begin moving into the streams to spawn. Some enter the streams in spring, but most do not move in until summer. Spawning takes place in fall, usually when the water temperature is in the low 40s. The female digs a redd on a bottom of medium to large gravel where there is moderate current. After spawning, the adults move to connecting lakes to spend the winter. Fewer than half live to spawn again.

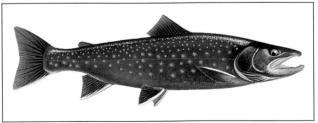

SPAWNING MALE DOLLY VARDEN — Back and sides dark brownish to greenish with pink or red spots, belly reddish orange, lower fins dark red to black. Lower jaw has strong kype.

17-inch Dolly Varden eating salmon eggs — Big Creek, Alaska

Age and Growth — Dollies have been known to live 19 years. They grow fastest in the northern part of their range.

Typical Length (inches) at Various Ages

Age	1	2	3	4	5	6	7	8	9
North	3.5	6.1	8.7	11.8	15.2	16.9	18.5	19.9	21.2
South	3.7	6.5	9.3	11.5	12.7	14.0	15.6	17.7	18.2

Typical Weight (pounds) at Various Lengths (inches)

Length	8	10	12	14	16	18	20
Weight	.21	.36	.56	.83	1.4	1.7	2.1

World Record — 10 pounds, 2 ounces, caught in the Kenai River, Alaska, in 1985. Dollies up to 12 pounds have been reported, but none have been authenticated since 1982, when the previous Dolly Varden record was dropped (page 51).

SPAWNING MALE ARCTIC CHAR — Greenish to brownish back and upper sides with pink or red spots, lower sides brilliant reddish

Arctic Char *(Salvelinus alpinus)*

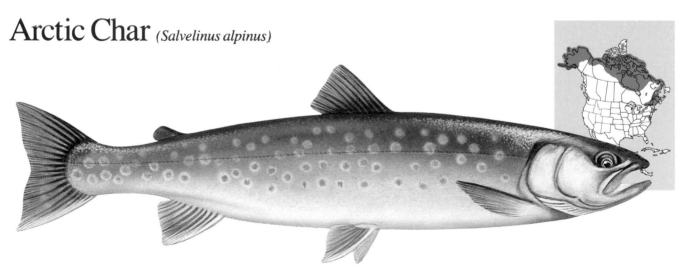

Common Names — Sea-run fish are also called silver char and ilkalupik (Eskimo name). In the East, landlocked forms are known as blueback trout, Quebec red trout or Marston trout, and Sunapee trout or Sunapee golden trout. In Alaska, most fishermen and even some biologists do not bother to differentiate between Arctic char and Dolly Varden, referring to either of them simply as char.

Description — Slightly forked tail, head without spots. Color highly variable, but normally silvery green on the sides with large pink, red or cream-colored spots, the largest at least as large as the pupil of the eye. The lower fins have white leading edges.

Forms — Biologists do not agree on the number of subspecies, but there are two widely recognized forms of Arctic char in North America. The anadromous form enters rivers draining to the Arctic Ocean and the Bering Sea. It is also found in inland lakes in the Arctic. The landlocked form is found mainly in oligotrophic lakes of northern New England, southern Quebec and southwest Alaska. Landlocked char are usually smaller but more colorful.

orange. Lower fins bright red. Lower jaw has a slight kype. Pictured: 14-pound spawning male — Tree River, Northwest Territories.

Hybrids — Arctic char occasionally hybridize with lake trout and brook trout.

Table Quality — The flesh varies from white to red, depending on the fish's diet. The red flesh is most desirable; some consider it even better than the finest salmon in flavor and texture.

Sporting Qualities — Powerful fighters; small char may jump several times when hooked, but big ones seldom jump. They can be caught on streamers and occasionally on dry flies, but a flashy spoon is considered most effective. Arctic char are not as wary as most other salmonids, so they are fairly easy to catch.

Habitat — Arctic char have a more northerly distribution than any other freshwater gamefish. Anadromous populations migrate upstream in late summer, spawning and wintering in the stream or an inland lake, then returning to sea the following spring. At sea, they usually remain in the vicinity of the stream mouth. Landlocked char use the same deep-water habitat as lake trout. They prefer water temperatures of 45° to 50°F.

Food Habits — They eat whatever is available to them, from plankton to small codfish to young of their own kind.

Spawning Habits — Char begin to appear in spawning streams in late summer. On an incoming tide, you can see them jumping and rolling. They spawn in fall, normally when the water drops to 39°F. The spawning site is usually a gravelly or rocky shoal in a lake, or a quiet pool in a river. The female digs a redd and the eggs hatch the following spring. Most landlocked char spawn on reefs similar to those used by lake trout, but some spawn in tributary streams.

Age and Growth — Arctic char grow very slowly, but may live as long as 40 years. They grow very little past age 20. Males grow faster than females. Landlocked char grow more slowly than sea-runs.

Typical Length (inches) at Various Ages

Age	2	4	6	8	10	12	14	16
Sea-run	—	14.4	17.2	19.7	22.0	25.3	26.7	28.5
Landlocked	5.5	10.6	15.2	18.5	18.8	19.3	20.0	—

Typical Weight (pounds) at Various Lengths (inches)

Length	12	15	18	21	24	27	30	33
Weight	0.6	1.5	2.5	4.0	6.4	8.5	11.7	16.9

World Record — Sea-run: 32 pounds, 9 ounces, taken in the Tree River, Northwest Territories, in 1981. Landlocked: 11 pounds, 8 ounces, caught in Sunapee Lake, New Hampshire, in 1954.

Florida bluegills — Rainbow River, Florida

Sunfish Family

The technical name of the sunfish family is *Centrarchidae,* meaning "nest builders." The males of each species construct a nest, guard the eggs from predators, and guard the fry until they leave the nest.

All members of the family are warmwater fish. They inhabit ponds, sloughs, slow-moving streams, shallow lakes, shallow bays of deeper lakes, and practically any other kind of warmwater habitat.

The sunfish family includes three major groups: true sunfish, crappies and black bass. Fliers, rock bass and Sacramento perch also belong to the sunfish family.

TRUE SUNFISH. This group of panfish includes members of the genus *Lepomis.* Their bright, colorful appearance accounts for the name "sunfish."

True sunfish are extremely popular with fishermen. They are easy to catch, good to eat, and wage an amazingly strong fight for their size. But in many waters they tend to overpopulate and become stunted.

Hybridization is very common among these fish. Hybrids are so predominant in some waters that you seldom see a purebred.

CRAPPIES. It would be difficult to say whether crappies (genus *Pomoxis*) or true sunfish are the most popular panfish. They inhabit the same types of water, although crappies will tolerate lower oxygen levels. As a result, crappies often become the most abundant species in winterkill lakes.

Unlike most other members of the sunfish family, crappies are roamers. They may be difficult to locate because of their habit of suspending far above bottom.

BLACK BASS. This group includes members of the genus *Micropterus.* The term "black bass" is derived from the black coloration of smallmouth bass fry.

Black bass, especially the largemouth and smallmouth, rank among North America's favorite gamefish. They will strike a wide variety of surface and subsurface lures, and usually jump or tailwalk when hooked.

Largemouth and smallmouth have been widely stocked throughout the United States and southern Canada. When introduced to new waters they generally reproduce successfully, so no further stocking is necessary.

Sunfish Family — Species Identification Key

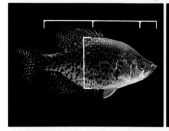 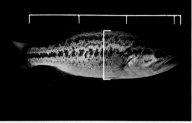

1 *Body (excluding fins) less than 3 times as long as it is deep . . . . go to 5* / *Body (excluding fins) at least 3 times as long as it is deep . . . . go to 2*

 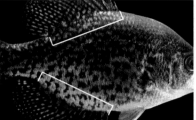

5 *Base of dorsal fin considerably longer than base of anal fin . . . . . . go to 7* / *Base of dorsal fin about same length as base of anal fin . . . . go to 6*

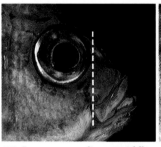 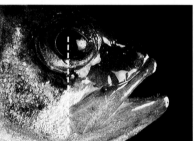

7 *Jaw not extending to middle of eye . . . . . . go to 10* / *Jaw extending at least to middle of eye . . . . go to 8*

10 *Pectoral fin not extending to anal fin . . go to 12* / *Pectoral fin extends to anal fin . . . . go to 11*

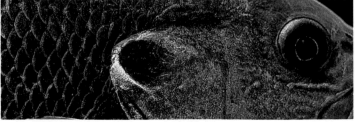

12 Gill-cover lobe no longer than deep . . . .
GREEN SUNFISH
Gill-cover lobe much longer than deep . . . . go to 13

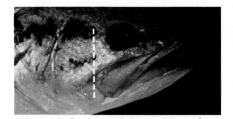

Short spine does not count as ray ↓

2 Jaw extends beyond rear of eye
LARGEMOUTH BASS

Jaw does not extend beyond rear of eye . . . . *go to 3*

3 Blotches on side connect to form a lateral band . . . SPOTTED BASS

No distinct lateral band . . . .
. . . . *go to 4*

4 12 soft-dorsal fin rays
REDEYE BASS   13 to 15 soft-dorsal fin rays
SMALLMOUTH BASS

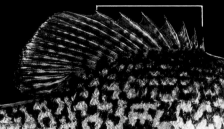

6 More than 10 dorsal spines . . . . . .
FLIER

7 or 8 dorsal spines . . . .
BLACK CRAPPIE

5 or 6 dorsal spines . . . .
WHITE CRAPPIE

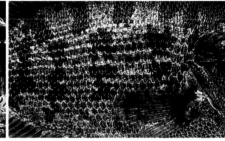

8 3 anal spines . . . . WARMOUTH
5 to 8 anal spines . . . . . . *go to 9*

9 Rows of dark spots along side . . . . .
ROCK BASS

Dark vertical bars on side . . . .
SACRAMENTO PERCH

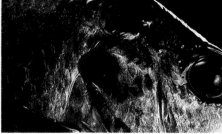

11 Gill-cover lobe black with no red
BLUEGILL

Reddish spot on lower part of gill-cover lobe . . . . PUMPKINSEED

Entire rear margin of gill-cover lobe red
REDEAR SUNFISH

13 Light-colored margin on gill-cover lobe . . . .
LONGEAR SUNFISH

No light-colored margin on gill-cover lobe . . . .
REDBREAST SUNFISH

SUNFISH FAMILY   59

Largemouth Bass
(Micropterus salmoides)

Northern largemouth bass

Common Names — Black bass, green bass, bigmouth and linesides.

Description — Light greenish to brownish sides with a dark lateral band that may come and go. The jaw extends well beyond the rear of the eye. Unlike spotted bass, there is no patch of teeth on the tongue.

Subspecies — Two are recognized: the northern largemouth *(Micropterus salmoides salmoides),* and the Florida largemouth *(Micropterus salmoides floridanus).* The two look much the same, but the Florida largemouth has slightly smaller scales in relation to the size of its body. It has 69 to 73 scales along the lateral line, compared to 59 to 65 on the northern largemouth. Originally, Florida largemouth were found only in peninsular Florida, but they have been stocked in several other states including Texas and California.

Table Quality — The meat is white, flaky and low in oil content. Largemouth taken from lakes where the predominant cover is weeds often have a grassy taste; those taken from clean water with woody cover usually have a mild flavor.

Sporting Qualities — The largemouth's liking for heavy cover makes it a challenge to land. A hooked largemouth usually heads for the surface, then opens its mouth wide, shaking its head or jumping in an attempt to throw the hook. Then it dives for cover and often wraps the line around logs, weeds or brush.

Largemouth will strike almost any kind of artificial lure or live bait, but most are taken on plastic worms, surface plugs, spinnerbaits, crankbaits, bass bugs and shiner minnows. The value of the largemouth as a sport fish has prompted a movement toward catch-and-release fishing.

Habitat — Largemouth thrive in eutrophic and mesotrophic natural lakes, especially those with plenty of submerged vegetation; reservoirs with an abundance of flooded timber and brush; ponds; pits; and slow-moving rivers and streams. They can tolerate a wide range of clarities and bottom types, and can even live in brackish water. They prefer water temperatures from 68° to 78°F, and are usually found at depths less than 20 feet.

Food Habits — Largemouth will eat whatever is available, including small fish, crayfish, larval and adult insects, mice, salamanders, leeches, frogs, snakes, and even turtles.

Spawning Habits — Spawn in spring at water temperatures from 63° to 68°F. The male sweeps away the silt to reach a firm sand or gravel bottom, usually along a shallow shoreline protected from the wind. Nests are often near weeds or logs. After spawning is completed, the male guards the eggs and later the fry, attacking anything that approaches the nest including crayfish, minnows, sunfish and fishermen's lures. Female Florida bass briefly share the nest-guarding duties with the male.

Age and Growth — In the North, largemouth may live as long as 16 years, but in the South they seldom exceed 10 years. Female largemouth live longer than males and are much more likely to reach trophy size. The northern subspecies grows only slightly faster in the South than in the North; the Florida subspecies grows considerably faster than the northern.

Typical Length (inches) at Various Ages

Age	1	2	3	4	5	6	8	10
Northern	4.7	8.5	11.3	13.4	15.3	17.1	19.5	20.8
Florida	7.5	12.0	15.5	18.2	20.3	22.1	24.9	—

Typical Weight (pounds) at Various Lengths (inches)

Length	12	14	16	18	20	22	24	26
Weight	1.0	1.9	2.7	3.5	5.4	7.2	8.6	9.5

World Record — 22 pounds, 4 ounces, caught in Montgomery Lake, Georgia, in 1932. This fish is thought to have been an intergrade between the two subspecies.

7-pound northern largemouth — Lake Hamilton, Arkansas

Spotted Bass *(Micropterus punctulatus)*

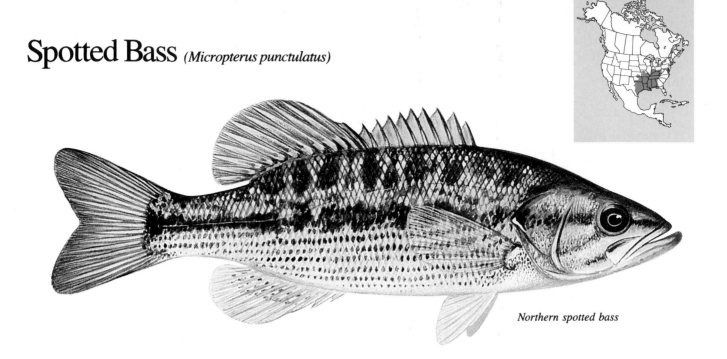

Northern spotted bass

Common Names — Kentucky bass, spot.

Description — Light green to light brown sides with a lateral band consisting of dark blotches, usually diamond-shaped. The jaw extends to the rear portion of the eye. Spotted bass have a distinct patch of teeth on the tongue (photo at right); largemouth do not.

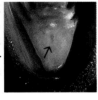

Subspecies — Two are recognized: the northern spotted bass *(Micropterus punctulatus punctulatus)*, and the Alabama spotted bass *(Micropterus punctulatus henshalli)*. The Wichita spotted bass *(Micropterus punctulatus wichitae)* is thought to be extinct.

The Alabama subspecies has a dark spot at the base of the tail and on the rear of the gill cover, and 68 to 75 scales along the lateral line. This subspecies is found only in Alabama, Mississippi and Georgia.

The northern subspecies also has a spot on the tail, but the spot on the gill cover is not as distinct, and there are only 60 to 68 scales along the lateral line. This is the subspecies found throughout most of the spotted bass range.

Hybrids — Spotted bass sometimes hybridize with smallmouth.

Table Quality — White, flaky meat with a good flavor. Generally considered better eating than largemouth.

Sporting Qualities — Although smaller and less acrobatic than smallmouth, spotted bass are strong fighters when caught on light tackle. Popular lures and baits include nymphs, jigs, crankbaits, spinners, small plastic worms, crayfish, spring lizards and hellgrammites.

Habitat — Spotted bass prefer small to medium-sized streams with clear, slow-moving water, and deep reservoirs. They are seldom found in natural lakes. In reservoirs, they inhabit deeper water than largemouth or smallmouth bass, sometimes retreating to depths of 100 feet. They prefer water temperatures in the mid-70s.

Food Habits — Crayfish are usually the most important item in the diet, followed by small fish, and larval and adult insects.

Spawning Habits — Spotted bass spawn in spring at water temperatures of about 63° to 68°F. Males sweep away silt from a gravel or rock bottom to make the nest, generally near brush, logs or other heavy cover. The males guard the eggs, and then guard the fry for up to a month after they leave the nest.

Age and Growth — The maximum life span, about 7 years, is much shorter than that of the smallmouth or largemouth, and the growth rate is slower.

Typical Length (inches) at Various Ages

Age	1	2	3	4	5	6	7
North	4.8	6.8	8.0	9.4	10.4	10.9	—
South	7.4	11.0	12.3	13.8	15.0	17.9	18.1

Typical Weight (pounds) at Various Lengths (inches)

Length	9	11	13	15	17	19
Weight	.33	.69	1.0	1.6	2.3	3.2

World Record — 9 pounds, 4 ounces, caught in Lake Perris, California, in 1987.

3-pound northern spotted bass — Lake Lanier, Georgia

Redeye Bass *(Micropterus coosae)*

ALABAMA REDEYE — Reddish dorsal, anal and caudal fins; upper sides often have blue spots, and the belly a bluish tinge. No dark spot at base of tail. Found in Alabama, Tennessee, Georgia and North Carolina.

Common Names — Coosa bass, shoal bass, Flint River smallmouth.

Description — The eyes are red, and the sides brownish to greenish, usually with vertical bars. There is a prominent dark spot on the gill cover. The jaw extends to the rear portion of the eye. Redeyes do not have a lateral band and resemble smallmouth more than largemouth. See descriptions of forms.

Forms — Although the taxonomy of the redeye-bass group is uncertain, there are two widely recog-

Alabama redeyes — Amacalola Creek, Georgia

nized forms: the Apalachicola form, or shoal bass, and the Alabama form.

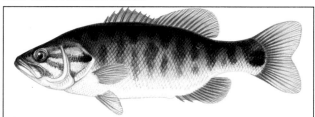

APALACHICOLA REDEYE (shoal bass) — Dark spot at base of tail, no blue spots on upper sides, fins not as intensely colored as in Alabama form. Found in the Apalachicola River system in Georgia, Alabama and Florida.

Table Quality — Good; the white, flaky meat is similar to that of smallmouth bass and somewhat drier than that of largemouth.

Sporting Qualities — Scrappy fighters, redeyes often jump when hooked. They can be caught on worms, minnows, hellgrammites and crayfish, as well as small spinners, nymphs, and a wide variety of small surface lures.

Habitat — Alabama redeyes are normally found in the headwaters of small streams, where the water may be too cold for other black bass. Shoal bass are more likely to be found in main-channel habitat.

Redeyes are seldom found in natural lakes, ponds or reservoirs. They prefer a water temperature of about 65°F.

Food Habits — Redeyes feed heavily on terrestrial insects on the surface. They also eat larval insects, crayfish and small fish.

Spawning Habits — Spawn in spring on coarse gravel at the head of a pool. Usual spawning temperature is 62° to 69°F. Males prepare the nest and guard the eggs and fry.

Age and Growth — Redeyes live as long as 10 years. The Alabama form grows very slowly; shoal bass grow much faster.

Typical Length (inches) at Various Ages

Age	1	2	3	4	5	6	7	8
Alabama	3.9	4.9	6.2	6.7	7.2	8.0	8.7	8.9
Shoal	3.8	8.1	11.4	13.9	15.3	18.9	20.7	21.5

Typical Weight (pounds) at Various Lengths (inches)

Length	8	10	12	14	16	18	20
Weight	.25	.47	.79	1.2	2.1	3.7	5.5

World Record — 8 pounds, 3 ounces, caught in the Flint River, Georgia, in 1977. This fish was a shoal bass.

Smallmouth Bass *(Micropterus dolomieui)*

NORTHERN SMALLMOUTH — Jaw extends to about middle of eye. No black spot at rear of gill cover (see Neosho small-mouth, opposite). Found in southern Canada, and in every state except Florida, Louisiana and Alaska.

Common Names — Bronzeback, brown bass, black bass, Oswego bass, green trout and redeye.

Description — Greenish to brownish sides with dark vertical bars that come and go. Three dark bars radiate from the eye. Smallmouth have a chameleonlike ability to change color. See subspecies descriptions.

Subspecies — Two are recognized: the northern smallmouth bass *(Micropterus dolomieui dolomieui),*

3-pound northern smallmouth — Grindstone Lake, Wisconsin

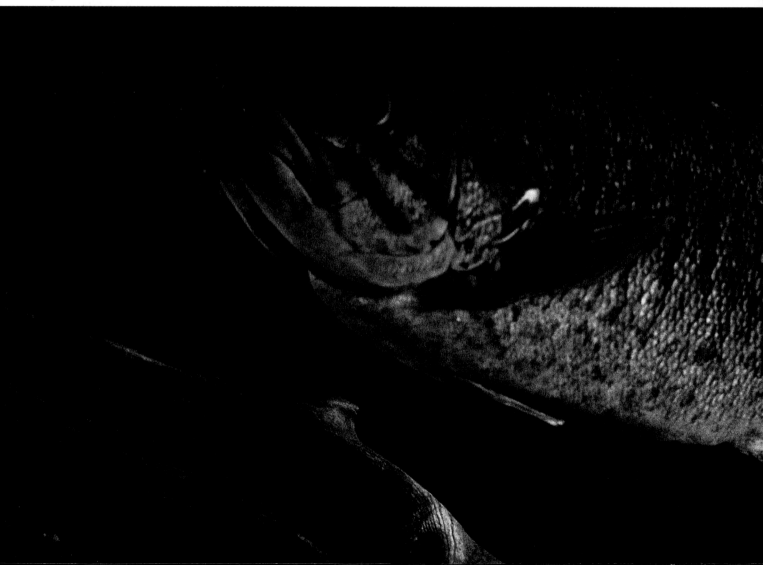

and the Neosho smallmouth bass *(Micropterus dolomieui velox)*. The latter is now rare because much of its native habitat was inundated after dams were constructed.

NEOSHO SMALLMOUTH — Prominent dark spot on rear of gill cover. Jaw extends slightly farther back than that of northern smallmouth, almost reaching rear of eye. Found mainly in tributaries of the Arkansas River in Oklahoma, Arkansas and Missouri.

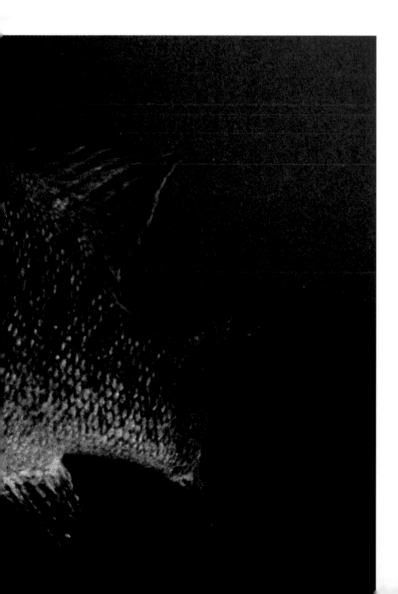

Hybrids — Known to hybridize with spotted bass.

Table Quality — The white, flaky flesh has an excellent flavor; it does not have the grassy taste that largemouth sometimes have.

Sporting Qualities — Considered by many to be the sportiest freshwater fish. Smallmouth are known for their fighting stamina and astounding leaping ability. Like largemouth, they will take almost any kind of lure or bait, but they generally prefer smaller sizes. Favorites include jigs, crankbaits, spinners, streamer flies, shiner minnows, crayfish, hellgrammites, leeches and nightcrawlers.

Habitat — Smallmouth like clean, clear water. They are found in all types of natural and manmade lakes, but are most common in mesotrophic lakes and mid-depth reservoirs. Smallmouth also thrive in rivers and streams with moderate current. Seldom are they found in small ponds, lakes shallower than 25 feet, or any water that is continuously murky or polluted. Smallmouth prefer water from 67° to 71°F. They do not compete well with other predatory fish.

Food Habits — Crayfish are the favored food, but smallmouth also eat larval and adult insects, frogs and tadpoles, and a variety of small fish.

Spawning Habits — Smallmouth spawn in spring, usually at water temperatures from 60° to 65°F. They can spawn successfully in streams or lakes. The male builds a nest by sweeping silt off a bottom of sand, gravel or rock. Usually the nest is protected by a boulder or log, and is not exposed to the wind. After spawning, the male guards the eggs. He continues to guard the fry for a week or two after they leave the nest.

Age and Growth — Smallmouth live up to 18 years in the North, seldom longer than 7 years in the South. But southern smallmouth grow much faster.

Typical Length (inches) at Various Ages

Age	1	2	3	4	5	6	7	8
North	4.2	6.7	8.6	10.9	13.0	14.6	15.8	16.9
South	5.9	10.7	13.5	16.6	18.5	20.4	21.0	21.6

Typical Weight (pounds) at Various Lengths (inches)

Length	12	14	16	18	20	22
Weight	1.0	1.5	2.6	3.9	5.0	6.2

World Record — 11 pounds, 15 ounces, caught in Dale Hollow Lake, Kentucky, in 1955.

Flier *(Centrarchus macropterus)*

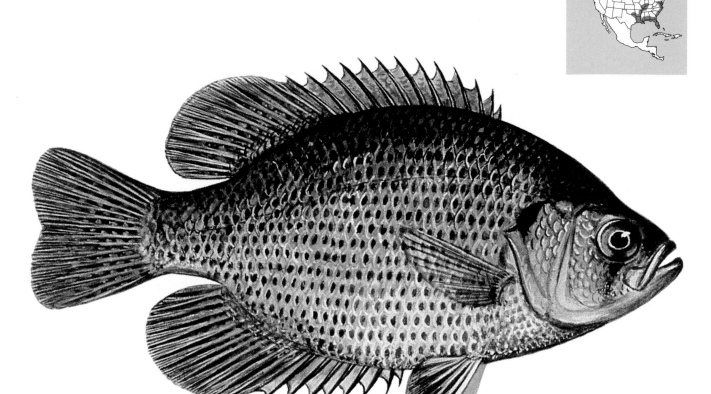

Common Name — Sometimes called round sunfish, because of its plate-like shape.

Description — Greenish to yellowish sides with a dark spot on each scale. There is usually a dusky streak extending below the eye. The dorsal fin has at least 11 spines, more than that of any other sunfish. Juveniles usually have a prominent black spot fringed in red at the rear of the dorsal, but the spot disappears as the fish mature.

Hybrids — Has been known to hybridize with white crappie.

Table Quality — Excellent; has white, flaky, sweet-tasting meat.

Sporting Qualities — Although fliers fight well for their size, they are often too small to generate much interest among anglers. Fliers can be caught on dry flies, tiny poppers, worms, insect larvae and small minnows.

Habitat — Fliers prefer heavily vegetated waters such as shallow lakes, sloughs, bayous and slow-moving streams. Often, they are found under mats of floating vegetation. Fliers can tolerate waters too acidic for other sunfish. They prefer water temperatures from 75° to 85°F.

Food Habits — Feed heavily on small crustaceans, but will eat mosquito larvae, other insects and small fish, particularly young-of-the-year bluegills.

Spawning Habits — Spawn earlier than other sunfish, usually at a water temperature of 62° to 64°F. Their habit of nesting in colonies provides a good fishing opportunity.

Age and Growth — Fliers live as long as 8 years, but grow very slowly.

Typical Length (inches) at Various Ages

Age	1	2	3	4	5	6	7	8
Length	2.2	3.6	4.8	5.8	6.5	7.1	7.3	7.8

Typical Weight (pounds) at Various Lengths (inches)

Length	5	6	7	8
Weight	.10	.14	.25	.41

World Record — No official record; the largest flier on record appears to be a 1-pound, 4-ounce fish caught in a South Carolina farm pond in 1978.

9-inch flier — Lake Chickahominy, Georgia

Black Crappie *(Pomoxis nigromaculatus)*

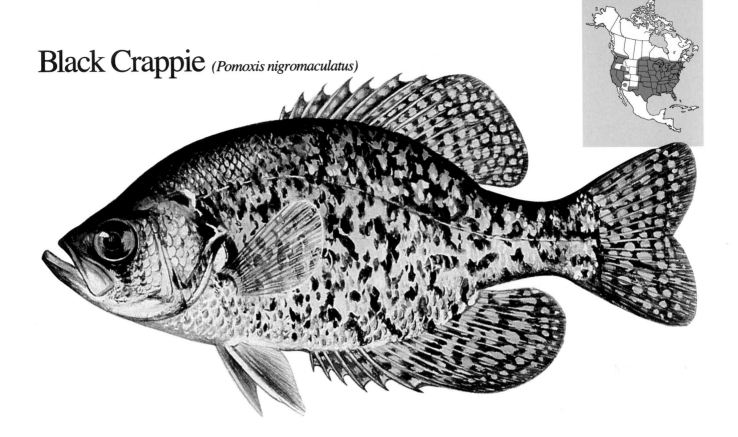

Common Names — Papermouth, speckled perch, bachelor perch, calico bass and strawberry bass.

Description — Silvery sides with a greenish to yellowish cast and scattered dark specks. The dorsal fin has 7 or 8 spines. Black crappies are deeper-bodied than whites and have a less noticeable depression in the profile above the eye.

Hybrids — Known to hybridize with white crappie.

Table Quality — The meat is white and tasty, but the texture is somewhat soft.

Sporting Qualities — Black crappies are better fighters than white crappies, but not nearly as strong as bluegills. The best live baits are small minnows and insect larvae. They will also strike subsurface flies, small spinners, jigs, and tiny crankbaits. Black crappies tend to suspend in midwater, so you may have to experiment to find the right depth.

Habitat — Black crappies prefer clearer water than whites. They thrive in clear, weedy natural lakes and reservoirs. They are also found in large, slow-moving rivers, provided the water is not too murky. Black crappies prefer water from 70° to 75°F, but will tolerate water over 80°.

SPAWNING MALE BLACK CRAPPIE (top) — Darker and more iridescent on head and breast than normal male. Spawning female (bottom) does not develop the dark coloration. Location: Ice Cracking Lake, Minnesota.

Food Habits — Plankton, small fish and larval aquatic insects make up most of the diet. Like white crappies, blacks spend a good deal of time feeding on suspended plankton in midwater.

Spawning Habits — Spawn in spring, usually at a water temperature of 62° to 65°F. They nest in colonies, with individual nests somewhat more apparent than the nests of white crappies. After spawning, males guard the eggs and fry.

Age and Growth — Black crappies live longer than whites, sometimes as long as 10 years. But they grow more slowly.

Typical Length (inches) at Various Ages

Age	1	2	3	4	5	6	7	8	9
North	2.9	5.5	7.4	8.6	9.1	10.4	11.6	11.9	12.6
South	3.1	6.7	9.0	10.6	11.3	11.7	12.6	12.8	13.8

Typical Weight (pounds) at Various Lengths (inches)

Length	8	9	10	11	12	13	14
Weight	.30	.51	.68	.84	1.0	1.5	2.4

World Record — 4 pounds, 8 ounces, caught in Kerr Lake, Virginia, in 1981. The previous world record of 6 pounds was dropped in 1985 because of insufficient verification.

White Crappie *(Pomoxis annularis)*

Common Names — Papermouth, speckled perch, bachelor perch, silver bass.

Description — Silvery sides with emerald and purple reflections and 7 to 9 dark vertical bars. The dorsal fin usually has 5 or 6 spines. White crappies are more elongated than black crappies and have a sharper depression in the profile just above the eye.

Hybrids — Hybridizes with black crappie and flier.

Table Quality — White meat with a good flavor but soft texture.

Sporting Qualities — Willing biters, white crappies will strike subsurface flies, small spinners, jigs and a wide variety of other artificials. The best live baits are small minnows and insect larvae. Schools of white crappies often suspend in midwater, so they may be difficult to locate. They are not strong fighters.

Habitat — White crappies thrive in natural and manmade lakes and in large, slow-moving rivers. They will tolerate murkier water than black crappies. They prefer water temperatures from 70° to 75°F, but can stand temperatures up to 85°.

Food Habits — Suspended plankton are an important part of the white crappie's diet. This explains why they spend so much time in midwater. Other important foods are small fish, fish eggs and larval aquatic insects.

Spawning Habits — Spawn on sand or gravel bottoms in spring, usually when the water temperature is 62° to 65°F. White crappies nest in colonies, but individual nests may not be apparent because there is no clean spot or depression. After spawning, males guard the eggs and fry.

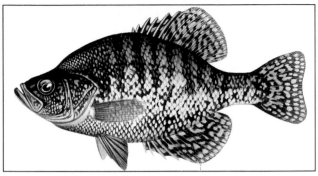

SPAWNING MALE WHITE CRAPPIE — Turns darker around the head and breast and the sides become more heavily spotted, sometimes as heavily as a spawning male black crappie.

Age and Growth — White crappies grow faster than blacks, but are shorter-lived. Few survive past age 8.

Typical Length (inches) at Various Ages

Age	1	2	3	4	5	6	7	8
North	5.6	7.2	8.7	9.9	10.6	11.0	11.7	13.1
South	3.8	6.0	8.2	9.8	11.9	13.2	14.3	15.4

Typical Weight (pounds) at Various Lengths (inches)

Length	8	9	10	11	12	13	14	15
Weight	.31	.44	.60	.75	1.0	1.3	1.8	2.3

World Record — 5 pounds, 3 ounces, caught at Enid Dam, Enid Lake, Mississippi, in 1957.

White crappies — Mississippi River backwaters, Iowa/Wisconsin border

Warmouth *(Lepomis gulosus)*

Common Names — Stumpknocker, goggle-eye and goggle-eyed perch.

Description — Resembles the rock bass because of its reddish eyes and olive-brown sides with brown mottling. But the anal fin has only 3 spines, compared to 6 on the rock bass, and there are several brownish streaks radiating from the eye.

Hybrids — Known to hybridize with bluegill, pumpkinseed, green sunfish, redbreast sunfish, and rock bass.

Table Quality — Good eating, but not popular as a food fish because of its small size.

Sporting Qualities — Easily caught in early season on subsurface flies and small poppers. Later, after the weed growth becomes heavy, you can catch warmouth by using a long cane pole or extension pole to dangle a worm or minnow in small pockets in the weeds. Warmouth are fairly good fighters, but not as strong as bluegills.

Habitat — Warmouth are found in shallow lakes, ponds, sloughs and slow-moving streams, with muddy bottoms and plenty of weeds, stumps, and logs for cover. They prefer water from 80° to 85°F, and can tolerate water up to 93°.

Food Habits — The diet consists of larval and adult insects, small fish, small crustaceans and snails.

Spawning Habits — Spawn in late spring or early summer at a water temperature of about 69°F. Males build a nest near a stump, rock or clump of vegetation. After spawning, they vigorously defend the nest until the fry leave. They have a unique method of scaring off intruders: their eyes turn bright red, and their bodies bright yellow.

Age and Growth — Warmouth live up to 8 years, but seldom reach a length over 11 inches.

Typical Length (inches) at Various Ages

Age	1	2	3	4	5	6
Length	3.3	4.9	6.2	6.9	7.3	7.7

Typical Weight (pounds) at Various Lengths (inches)

Length	6	7	8	9	10	11
Weight	.34	.40	.53	.75	.97	1.2

World Record — 2 pounds, 7 ounces, caught in Guess Lake, Florida, in 1985.

9-inch warmouth — Lochloosa Lake, Florida

Rock Bass *(Ambloplites rupestris)*

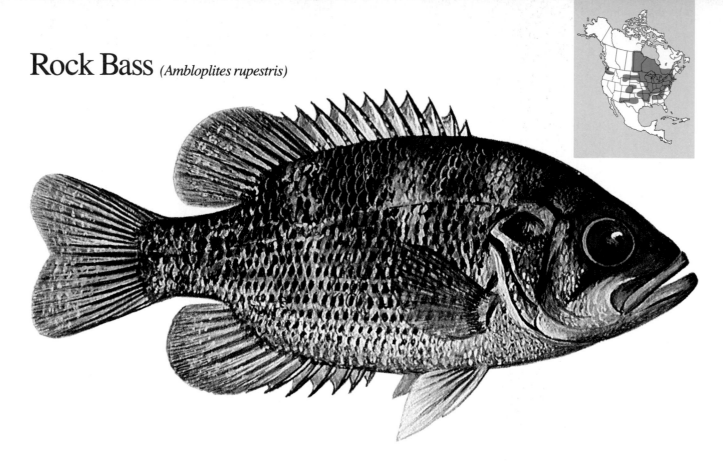

Common Names — Goggle-eye, redeye, and rock sunfish.

Description — Light brownish or greenish sides with brassy reflections and horizontal rows of dark spots. The eye is reddish, and the anal fin has 6 spines. Rock bass are adept at changing their color to blend with their surroundings.

Subspecies — Currently no subspecies are recognized. At one time, the deeper-bodied shadow bass *(Ambloplites ariommus)* was considered a subspecies of rock bass.

Hybrids — Hybrids between rock bass and shadow bass have been found in some parts of the South. Rock bass also hybridize with the warmouth and bluegill.

Table Quality — The flavor is good, but the meat is sometimes infested with parasites, especially in clear northern lakes.

Sporting Qualities — Rock bass are willing biters, striking with the force of fish twice their size. But they are not particularly strong fighters, and often spin in tight circles when reeled in. They will strike flies, jigs, spinners, crankbaits, minnows, worms, leeches, crayfish, hellgrammites and a wide variety of other lures and baits.

Habitat — Rock bass prefer clear, weedy lakes and ponds, and clear, slow-moving streams. They are usually found over a rocky bottom; seldom over a silty one. Preferred temperature range: 69° to 74°F.

Food Habits — Aquatic insects, crayfish and small fish make up the bulk of the diet. Rock bass do most of their feeding near bottom, but will take adult insects off the surface.

Spawning Habits — Spawn in late spring or early summer at water temperatures in the upper 60s. The male builds the nest in very shallow water, usually over a coarse sand or gravel bottom. After spawning, he guards the eggs and fry.

Age and Growth — Rock bass grow slowly, but may live up to 13 years. Males grow somewhat faster than females.

Typical Length (inches) at Various Ages

Age	1	2	3	4	5	7	9	11
North	1.6	2.8	3.9	4.9	5.9	7.7	8.7	9.3
South	2.3	4.6	6.3	7.4	7.8	9.0	—	—

Typical Weight (pounds) at Various Lengths (inches)

Length	6	7	8	9	10	11	12
Weight	.16	.25	.39	.57	.79	.92	1.2

World Record — 3 pounds, caught in the York River, Ontario, in 1974.

SPAWNING MALE ROCK BASS — Dark head; black margin on anal fin. Location: Round Lake, Minnesota.

Sacramento Perch *(Archoplites interruptus)*

Description — Light brown sides with greenish to purplish reflections, 6 or 7 irregular dark bars along the side, and a dark spot on the gill-cover lobe.

Table Quality — White, flaky meat with a good flavor.

Sporting Qualities — Because they seldom form schools and are not aggressive feeders, Sacramento perch are more difficult to catch than most other panfish. The best time to fish for them is when they congregate to spawn. They will strike subsurface flies, jigs, spinners, small crankbaits and minnows. A slow retrieve usually works best.

Habitat — Sacramento perch are usually found in weedy lakes, sloughs and sluggish rivers. They can tolerate highly alkaline waters, and have been stocked in prairie lakes with salinities too high for most other gamefish. They prefer water temperatures from 65° to 75°F.

Food Habits — The diet consists mostly of insect larvae, small crustaceans and small fish, including their own young. They will also take beetles, water boatmen and other adult insects off the surface.

Spawning Habits — Spawn in late spring or early summer, usually at water temperatures from 70° to 75°F. The males do not build nests, but select a definite spawning site, normally in a weedy area shared by many other spawners. After spawning, the parents abandon the eggs, leaving them vulnerable to predators. This habit has led to a decline of Sacramento perch populations in waters where other fish have been stocked.

Age and Growth — Sacramento perch have a maximum life span of about 9 years. Females grow faster and normally live longer than males.

Typical Length (inches) at Various Ages

Age	1	2	3	4	5	7	9
Length	4.2	7.5	8.8	9.6	11.0	12.6	14.9

Typical Weight (pounds) at Various Lengths (inches)

Length	8	9	10	11	12	13	14	15	16
Weight	.45	.51	.60	.75	.91	1.3	1.8	2.4	3.0

World Record — No official world record. A 4-pound, 9-ounce Sacramento perch was caught in Pyramid Lake, Nevada, in 1971.

12- to 14-inch Sacramento perch — Crowley Lake, California

Bluegill
(Lepomis macrochirus)

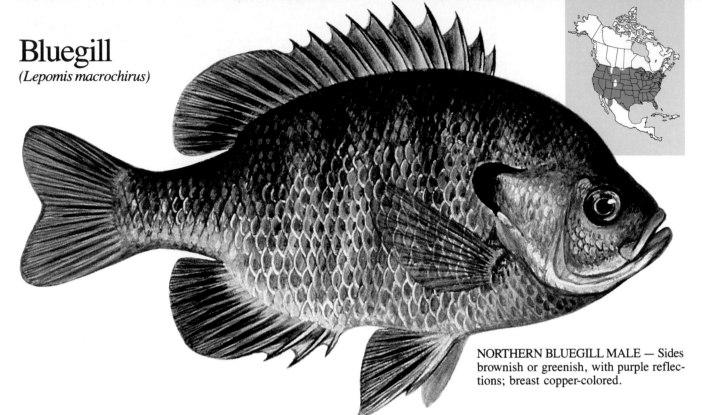

NORTHERN BLUEGILL MALE — Sides brownish or greenish, with purple reflections; breast copper-colored.

Common Names — Sun perch, bream, blue sunfish, copperbelly, roach.

Description — The gill cover has a powder-blue fringe, and the gill-cover lobe is entirely black. The sides have about 5 dark, vertical bars, that may be vague. The rear base of the dorsal fin has a dark blotch. The pectoral fin is long and sharply pointed. See subspecies descriptions.

NORTHERN BLUEGILL FEMALE — Sides somewhat lighter than the male's; breast yellowish rather than copper-colored.

Subspecies — Two are recognized: the northern bluegill *(Lepomis macrochirus macrochirus)*, found throughout the bluegill range except peninsular Florida; and the Florida bluegill *(Lepomis macrochirus mystacalis)*, found in Florida except in the panhandle.

FLORIDA BLUEGILL — Dark bluish to greenish on the back, sides lighter. Males (shown above) have a coppery patch above the eye that becomes more distinct at spawning time.

Hybrids — Hybridizes with redear, longear, redbreast, and green sunfish, and with pumpkinseed, warmouth, and rock bass.

Table Quality — Superb; the meat is white, flaky, firm and sweet. Many rank the bluegill as the most delicious of all freshwater fish.

Sporting Qualities — When a you hook a bluegill, it turns its body broadside and swims in circles, pulling as hard as other fish twice its size. Bluegills will strike poppers and dry flies as well as subsurface flies, tiny jigs and spinners, sponge spiders, and a wide variety of live bait including worms, leeches, tiny minnows, grass shrimp, crickets, grasshoppers and grubs.

Habitat — The best bluegill populations occur in clear waters with moderate weed growth, such as shallow, weed-fringed lakes and slow-moving portions of streams. If there are too many weeds, bluegills tend to become stunted. Large bluegills are usually found in deeper water than small ones. Bluegills prefer water temperatures from 75° to 80°F.

Food Habits — A bluegill's diet consists mainly of larval and adult insects, plankton, snails, and fish fry. They sometimes eat aquatic plants. Bluegills will take food on the surface, in the middle depths or on the bottom.

Spawning Habits — Spawn in spring, most commonly at water temperatures from 68° to 70°F. Some spawning continues into the summer. Spawning activity is heaviest a few days either side of the full moon. The male builds a nest on a sand or gravel bottom, often near other bluegill nests. After spawning, he guards the eggs and fry.

Northern bluegill taking insect — Sunrise Lake, Minnesota

NORTHERN BLUEGILL SPAWNING MALE — Overall coloration darkens, and copper color on breast becomes more intense. On large males, hump ahead of dorsal fin becomes more noticeable.

Age and Growth — Bluegills live up to 11 years. The rate of growth varies considerably in different bodies of water.

Typical Length (inches) at Various Ages

Age	1	2	3	4	5	6	7	8	9
North	3.8	5.0	5.6	6.3	7.1	7.7	8.1	8.5	8.6
South	4.7	5.7	6.7	7.6	8.1	9.3	—	—	—

Typical Weight (pounds) at Various Lengths (inches)

Length	6	7	8	9	10
Weight	.22	.35	.50	.68	1.0

World Record — 4 pounds, 12 ounces, caught in Ketona Lake, Alabama, in 1950.

Pumpkinseed
(Lepomis gibbosus)

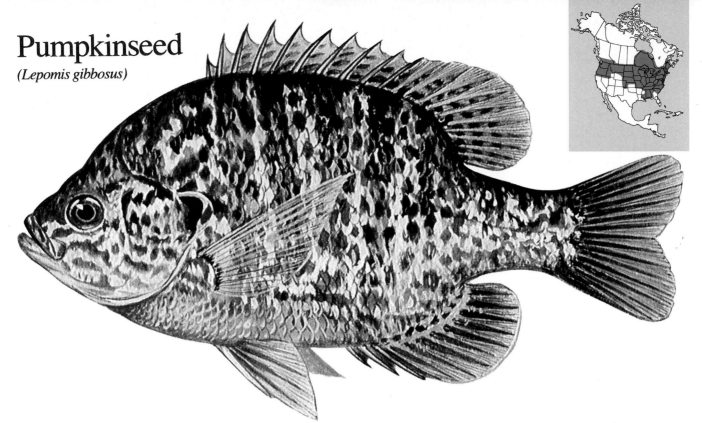

Common Names — Common sunfish, yellow sunfish, bream.

Description — Gold sides with 7 to 10 faint vertical bars which tend to be more prominent on females. The sides often have blue and emerald reflections and green, orange, or red flecks. The cheeks have wavy bluish streaks, and the gill-cover lobe has an orange or red spot at the tip.

Hybrids — Commonly hybridizes with bluegill; less commonly with redbreast, redear, green, and longear sunfish, and with warmouth.

Table Quality — White, flaky, sweet-tasting meat, very similar to that of a bluegill.

Sporting Qualities — Easy to catch; will take almost any small live bait, including worms, grubs, grasshoppers and leeches. Pumpkinseeds have small mouths, so they tend to nibble the bait. Good lures include fly-rod poppers, wet flies, small spinners, and tiny twister-tail jigs. Pumpkinseeds are good fighters, but not quite as determined as bluegills.

Habitat — Pumpkinseeds thrive in small, shallow lakes, sheltered bays of larger lakes, and quiet areas of slow-moving streams. They are normally found in shallower water and denser vegetation than bluegills and redears. Because they can tolerate cooler water temperatures than other sunfish, their range extends farther north. They prefer water temperatures from 70° to 75°F.

Food Habits — Adult and larval insects make up most of the diet, but pumpkinseeds also eat snails and fish fry.

Spawning Habits — Spawn in late spring or early summer, usually at water temperatures from 66° to 70°F. Males build the nests on a sand or fine gravel bottom at depths from 6 to 18 inches. After spawning, males guard the eggs and fry. In one study, males were seen apparently eating fry that had strayed from the nest, but closer observation revealed that they carried the fry back and spat them out on the nest.

Age and Growth — Pumpkinseeds may live up to 10 years. They grow slightly faster in the northern states and Canada than in the southern part of their range, probably because of their preference for cooler water. Males grow somewhat faster than females.

Typical Length (inches) at Various Ages

Age	1	2	3	4	5	6	7	8	9
Length	2.6	4.3	4.9	5.4	6.3	7.0	7.5	8.1	8.3

Typical Weight (pounds) at Various Lengths (inches)

Length	5	6	7	8	9
Weight	.13	.25	.35	.50	.72

World Record — 1 pound, 6 ounces, caught in Oswego Pond, New York, in 1985.

SPAWNING MALE PUMPKINSEED — Overall coloration becomes darker and more intense. Yellowish gold color on breast changes to orange. Location: Big Toad Lake, Minnesota.

Redear Sunfish *(Lepomis microlophus)*

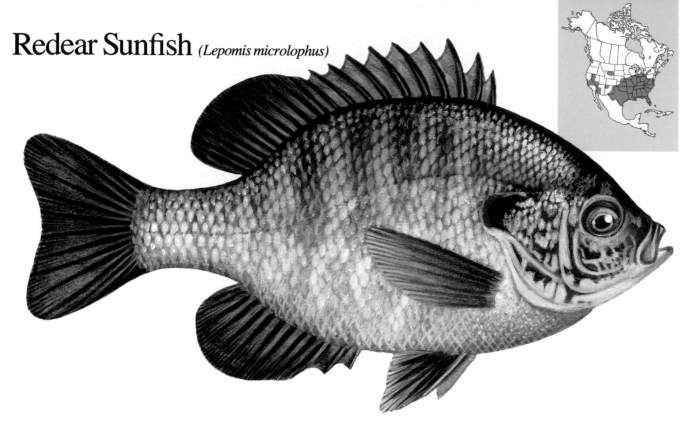

Common Names — Widely known as shellcracker because of its fondness for snails. Also called stumpknocker, bream and yellow bream.

Description — The sides are light olive-green to gold, with red or orange flecks. The black gill-cover lobe has a bright red or orange margin. Redears resemble pumpkinseeds, but are less colorful and lack the bluish streaks on the cheeks. Males and females are similar in appearance.

Hybrids — Known to hybridize with bluegill and pumpkinseed, and with longear and green sunfish.

Table Quality — Similar to that of bluegill, with white, flaky, sweet-tasting meat.

Sporting Qualities — Strong fighters, but more difficult to catch than most other sunfish. Live bait, especially worms, crickets, grubs, catalpa worms and shrimp, usually works better than artificial lures. Most redears are caught on the spawning beds. Later in the season they move to much deeper water or into heavy cover, where they are difficult to locate.

Habitat — Redears prefer clear, quiet water with moderate vegetation. Rarely are they found in moving water. They tolerate brackish water better than other sunfish but are intolerant of cool water. Preferred water temperature: 73° to 77°F.

Food Habits — Important food items include snails, which are crushed by the grinding teeth in the throat; larval insects; and fish eggs.

Spawning Habits — Spawn in late spring or early summer, generally at water temperatures from 66° to 70°F. Males build nests on sand-gravel bottoms or on softer bottoms along the edge of lily pads or submerged weeds. The male guards the eggs, then guards the fry for about a week after they hatch.

SPAWNING MALE REDEAR — Overall coloration becomes more intense. Breast becomes bright yellow or yellow-orange.

Age and Growth — Redears grow faster than any other true sunfish. The maximum age is about 8 years.

Typical Length (inches) at Various Ages

Age	1	2	3	4	5	6	7
Length	4.8	6.8	7.2	8.1	9.4	10.0	10.3

Typical Weight (pounds) at Various Lengths (inches)

Length	6	7	8	9	10	11	12	13
Weight	.18	.28	.40	.63	.91	1.2	1.6	2.3

World Record — 4 pounds, 13 ounces, caught in Merritt's Mill Pond, Florida, in 1986.

11-inch redear — Lake Chickahominy, Georgia

SPAWNING MALE GREEN SUNFISH — Color becomes darker and more intense; fins develop light margins.

Green Sunfish *(Lepomis cyanellus)*

Location: Lake Cornelia, Minnesota.

Common Names — Green perch, blue-spotted sunfish, rubbertail and bream.

Description — Dark olive on the back; lighter olive on the sides with iridescent green or blue flecks; cheek has iridescent green or blue streaks. The gill-cover lobe has a light rear margin. The sides often have 7 to 12 faint dark, vertical bars. The mouth is large and the body more elongated than that of most other true sunfish. Both sexes are similar in appearance.

Hybrids — Green sunfish hybridize with bluegill, pumpkinseed, and warmouth, and with redear, redbreast and longear sunfish.

Table Quality — White, flaky, good-tasting meat, similar to that of a bluegill.

Sporting Qualities — Green sunfish are easy to catch and fight fairly well, but are too small to be highly regarded as gamefish. Most are caught by anglers fishing for other sunfish with flies, small spinners and worms.

Habitat — Usually found in heavy cover such as large rocks, brush piles or thick weeds. They can tolerate murky water, low oxygen levels and silty bottoms. Green sunfish live in slow-moving streams, ponds, and shallow, weedy bays of lakes. They prefer warm water, from 80° to 84°F.

Food Habits — Because of their sizable mouths, green sunfish can eat large food items. Aquatic and terrestrial insects, crayfish and small fish make up the bulk of their diet.

Spawning Habits — Spawn in late spring and early summer, usually at water temperatures of 69° to 73°F. Males build nests on fine gravel bottoms, generally beneath limbs or other cover. After spawning, males guard the eggs and fry.

Age and Growth — Green sunfish grow slowly and tend to become stunted. Few live beyond 6 years. Males grow faster and live longer than females.

Typical Length (inches) at Various Ages

Age	1	2	3	4	5	6
North	2.3	3.4	4.2	4.6	5.5	6.5
South	3.5	4.6	5.8	6.9	7.4	9.1

Typical Weight (pounds) at Various Lengths (inches)

Length	5	6	7	8	9	10
Weight	.15	.23	.30	.39	.48	.67

World Record — 2 pounds, 2 ounces, caught in Stockton Lake, Missouri, in 1971.

Longear Sunfish

(Lepomis megalotis)

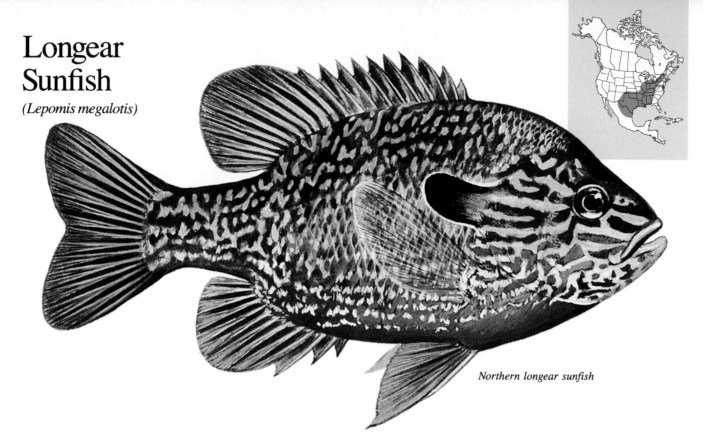

Northern longear sunfish

Common Names — Red-bellied bream, red perch, blackear and bream.

Description — The sides are mottled with orange and iridescent turquoise; the cheeks have iridescent turquoise streaks. The long, black gill-cover lobe accounts for the name "longear." The lobe has a light-colored margin.

Subspecies — Two are recognized. The central longear *(Lepomis megalotis megalotis)* has a very long gill-cover lobe that is almost horizontal. The margin of the lobe sometimes has several small, reddish spots. This subspecies reaches a maximum size of about 9 inches. Central longears are the predominant subspecies, and are found throughout most of the longear sunfish range.

The northern longear *(Lepomis megalotis peltastes)* has a shorter gill-cover lobe that extends upward at a 45-degree angle. The margin of the lobe often has a single red or orange spot. This subspecies grows to a maximum size of about 5 inches. Northern longears are found in the southern Great Lakes and connecting waters.

Hybrids — Hybridizes with redear and green sunfish, and with bluegill and pumpkinseed.

Table Quality — The white, flaky, sweet-tasting meat is considered excellent eating.

Sporting Qualities — Small but feisty, the longear is usually caught on natural baits such as worms, crickets, minnows and small crayfish. It will also strike small flies and spinners.

Habitat — Longears are most common in clear, shallow, slow-moving streams with moderate vegetation and a sand, gravel or rubble bottom. They are occasionally found in warmwater lakes, reservoirs and ponds. They prefer water from 75° to 80°F, but can survive at temperatures up to 100°.

Food Habits — Longears feed mainly on immature aquatic insects, worms, crayfish and fish eggs. They sometimes take adult insects on the surface.

Spawning Habits — Spawn in summer, normally at water temperatures from 70° to 74°F, but sometimes as high as 85°. Males build nests over a gravel bottom, often in colonies. After spawning, males guard the nests until the fry disperse.

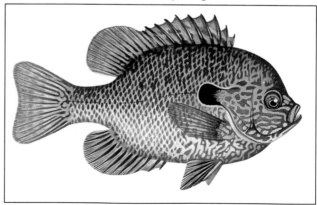

SPAWNING MALE LONGEAR (central subspecies) — Bluish or greenish spots on back and upper sides become almost fluorescent; flanks and belly an intense rusty orange.

Age and Growth — The maximum age is 9 years, but few live beyond age 6. The relatively short life

Central longear sunfish — Lake Ouachita, Arkansas

span and slow growth rate account for the longear's small size.

Typical Length (inches) at Various Ages

Age	1	2	3	4	5	6
Northern	1.5	2.4	2.7	3.0	3.6	4.3
Central	3.2	4.4	4.8	5.3	5.9	6.0

Typical Weight (pounds) at Various Lengths (inches)

Length	4	5	6	7	8	9
Weight	.10	.13	.24	.35	.50	.71

World Record — 1 pound, 12 ounces, caught in Elephant Butte Lake, New Mexico, in 1985.

Redbreast Sunfish

(Lepomis auritus)

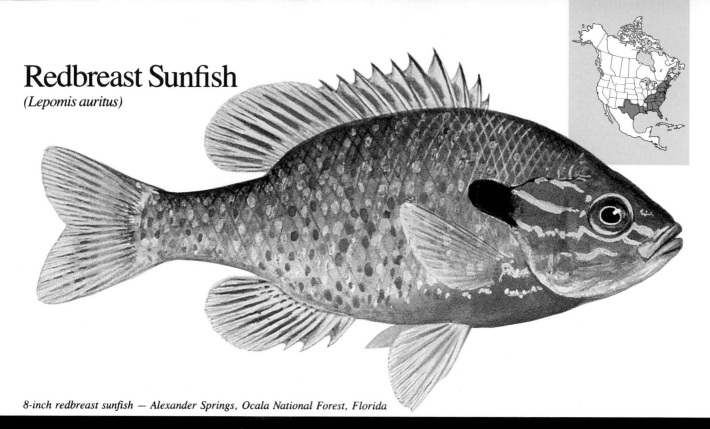

8-inch redbreast sunfish — Alexander Springs, Ocala National Forest, Florida

Common Names — Yellowbelly sunfish, robin, redbelly and bream.

Description — The black gill-cover lobe of a redbreast is as long as that of the central longear sunfish, but there is no light-colored margin. Males have a reddish breast, olive upper sides and blue streaks on the cheek. Females are less colorful; their breasts are yellowish or pale red.

Hybrids — Known to hybridize with warmouth, bluegill, pumpkinseed and green sunfish.

Table Quality — The white, flaky, sweet-tasting meat is considered excellent eating.

Sporting Qualities — Redbreasts are prized gamefish in parts of the South, but in the northern part of their range, they are too small to generate much interest. They are spunky fighters and will bite on flies and small spinners, as well as worms, crickets, grasshoppers and small minnows. Unlike most sunfish, redbreasts bite well at night.

Habitat — Found mostly in streams along coastal plains, although they also live in lakes and ponds. They prefer deep, slow-moving areas of streams. They usually hide behind boulders or logs, or in undercut tree roots. Redbreasts prefer warm water, from 80° to 84°F.

Food Habits — Common foods include aquatic and terrestrial insects, snails, crayfish and small fish.

Spawning Habits — Spawn in late spring or early summer, usually at water temperatures from 66° to 70°F, but sometimes at temperatures as high as 82°. Males build nests on sand or gravel bottoms, generally near stumps, rocks or logs. The males guard the nests until shortly after the fry hatch.

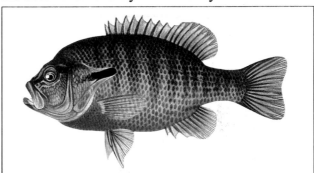

SPAWNING MALE REDBREAST — Overall coloration darkens; reddish color on breast becomes much more vivid.

Age and Growth — Compared to most other sunfish, redbreasts grow slowly. They seldom live beyond 7 years.

Typical Length (inches) at Various Ages

Age	1	2	3	4	5	6
North	2.2	2.9	3.3	3.9	4.3	5.4
South	3.0	4.7	5.6	6.5	7.1	7.4

Typical Weight (pounds) at Various Lengths (inches)

Length	4	5	6	7	8
Weight	.05	.10	.17	.27	.40

World Record — 1 pound, 12 ounces, caught in the Suwannee River, Florida, in 1984. A 2-pound redbreast was caught in the Lumber River, South Carolina, in 1975, but was never officially recognized.

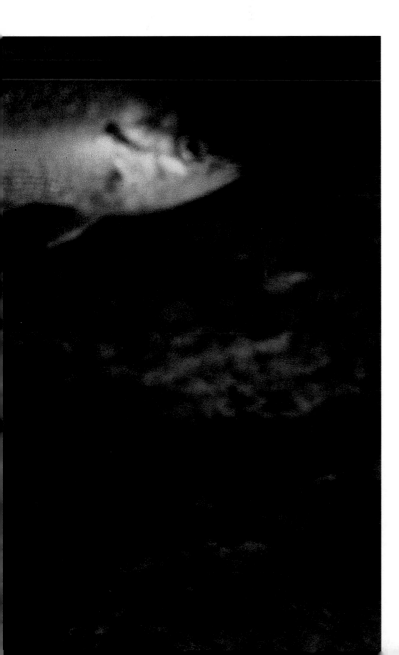

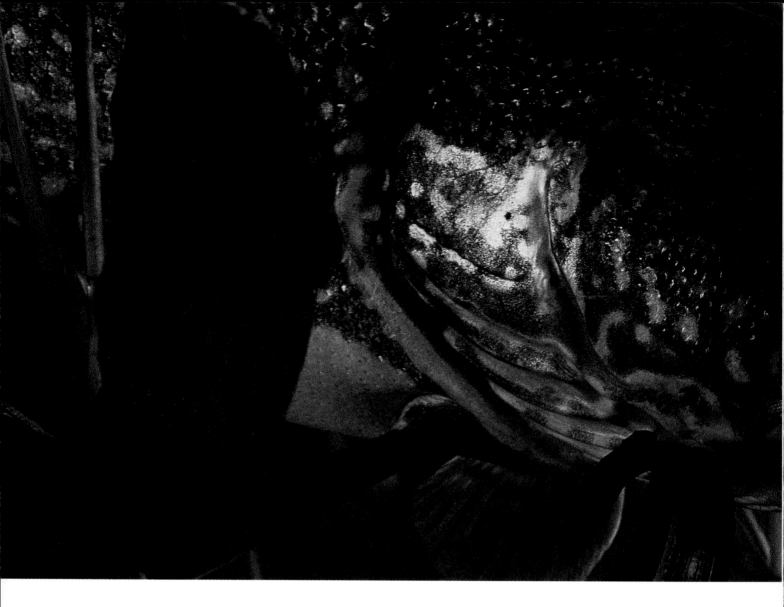

Pike Family

The highly carnivorous habits of these gamefish have inspired thousands of "fish stories," ranging from swimmers being bitten while dangling their toes in the water to small dogs being eaten while going for a swim. Most of these stories result from overactive imaginations, but some are true.

The pike family *(Esocidae)* includes only one genus, *Esox,* and four species in North America. Northern pike, muskellunge and chain pickerel enjoy widespread popularity among anglers, but redfin pickerel are often too small to generate much interest.

All members of the pike family have long bodies; snouts shaped like a duck's bill; large, needle-sharp teeth; and a dorsal fin far back on the body. Because of its elongated shape, a pike can contort its body into a slight "Z," then spring forward at amazing speed to attack unsuspecting prey.

Pike are random spawners rather than nest builders. They scatter their eggs in the shallows, then abandon them. The fry must fend for themselves, and they soon develop carnivorous habits. About three to four weeks after hatching, they begin cannibalizing other fry.

Because of their large mouths, pike can eat larger food items than other fish of the same size. A pike often grabs a fish one-third or even one-half of its own length. If it cannot swallow the fish whole, it swims around with the tail protruding from its mouth until the head has been digested. Then it swallows some more.

Knowledgeable fishermen take advantage of the pikes' liking for large foods by fishing with big baits and lures. Anglers who specialize in trophy-size northerns and muskies often use baitfish weighing a pound or more and lures measuring over a foot long. Experience has shown that these over-sized baits and lures will draw strikes from fish that ignore smaller offerings.

Northern pike eating sucker — Deer Lake, Minnesota

When fishing for any type of pike, always use a wire leader. Their sharp teeth will easily cut monofilament. Some fishermen maintain that 20- to 30-pound mono will prevent bite-offs, but a big pike can bite through it. Because of the pikes' aggressive nature, a wire leader will not reduce the number of strikes.

Pike Family — Species Identification Key

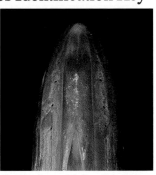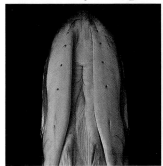

1 *Lower jaw with 10 or more pores* . . . . **go to 2**   *Lower jaw with 8 or less pores* . . . . **go to 3**

2 Dark background with light, bean-shaped spots . . **NORTHERN PIKE**   Light background, usually with dark spots or stripes . . . **MUSKELLUNGE**

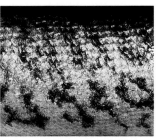

3 Chain-link marks on sides **CHAIN PICKEREL**   Wavy, vertical bars on sides . . **REDFIN PICKEREL**

Northern Pike *(Esox lucius)*

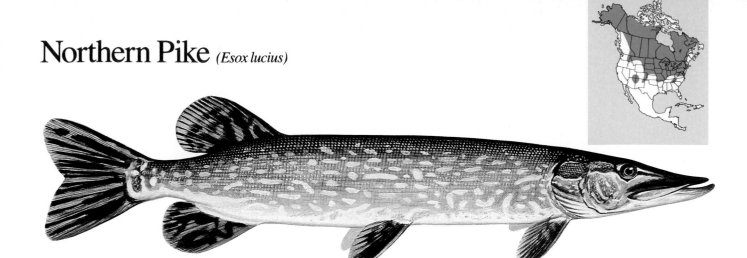

Common Names — Great northern pike, jack, jackfish, pickerel, snake, gator.

Description — The sides are dark green to olive-green with rows of light, oval spots. The fins have dark spots and often a reddish tinge. There are usually 10 pores on the underside of the lower jaw. The entire cheek and top half of the gill cover is scaled (photo at right).

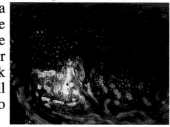

Hybrids — Northern pike sometimes hybridize with muskellunge, producing the tiger muskie (page 96). They also hybridize with chain and redfin pickerel. Occasionally, anglers catch a mutant form of northern pike, called silver pike, which ranges in color from metallic blue to bright silver.

SILVER PIKE — Silvery sides without any markings; scales usually flecked with silver or gold. Occurs occasionally throughout northern pike range.

Table Quality — The white, flaky meat has a good flavor, but each fillet has a row of Y-bones. By cutting around the bones, they can easily be removed.

Sporting Qualities — The northern's predatory nature makes it one of the easiest gamefish to catch. The best lures are big spoons, spinners and jerkbaits, but pike will attack any artificial that looks big enough for a meal. One of the most effective baits is a big minnow fished beneath a float. Any bait or lure should be fished with a wire leader so it will not be sheared off by the pike's sharp teeth. When hooked, northerns sometimes leap or thrash on the surface, then make a series of powerful runs.

Habitat — Northern pike can live in almost any type of fresh water, from shallow marshes to small coldwater streams. They reach greatest abundance in weedy bays of natural lakes and in slow, meandering rivers with heavy weed growth. As northerns grow larger, they require colder water. Those under 7 pounds prefer water from 65° to 70°F; larger ones, from 50° to 55°.

Food Habits — Northerns are opportunists, feeding on whatever they can find. Fish make up most of the diet, but they also eat frogs, crayfish, mice, muskrats and ducklings. As a rule, northerns prefer one large food item to several smaller ones.

Spawning Habits — Spawn in early spring, normally just after ice-out, but sometimes before the ice melts. Spawning takes place in small tributary streams or marshes adjacent to lakes, or in shallow weedy bays. The usual water temperature at spawning time is 40° to 45°F. The eggs are scattered at random, and the parents make no attempt to guard the young.

Age and Growth — Northerns are long-lived, with some fish in the far North reaching ages of 25 years. In the southern part of their range, few live beyond 6 years. Females grow faster and live longer than males.

Typical Length (inches) at Various Ages

Age	1	3	5	8	11	14	17	20
North	3.2	8.1	12.3	17.8	23.8	29.4	34.1	38.8
South	10.9	23.0	28.3	—	—	—	—	—

Typical Weight (pounds) at Various Lengths (inches)

Length	20	25	30	35	40	45
Weight	1.8	3.6	5.8	10.6	16.5	23.9

World Record — 46 pounds, 2 ounces, caught in Sacandaga Reservoir, New York, in 1940. Many larger northerns have been caught in Europe, but never verified as official records. One weighing 90 pounds, 8 ounces was caught in Loch Deigh, Ireland, in 1862.

14-pound northern pike — Pokegama Lake, Minnesota

Muskellunge *(Esox masquinongy)*

SPOTTED MUSKIE — Sides have rows of roundish dark spots or blotches on a lighter background.

Common Names — Muskie, lunge, maskinonge, great pike and more than forty other local names.

Description — Sometimes confused with northern pike, but the two species can easily be separated. The muskie has dark marks on a light background, while the northern has light marks on a dark background. Also, the tips of the muskie's tail are more pointed. The muskie's marks range from small spots to vertical bars, depending on the color phase. There are usually 12 to 18 pores on the underside of the lower jaw. The cheek and gill cover have scales only on the top half (photo at right). See descriptions of color phases.

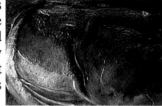

Color Phases — In the past, there were three recognized subspecies, but widespread stocking has mixed the genetic makeup of most populations. Today, most biologists recognize only one form of muskie. Nevertheless, there are three distinct color phases: spotted, barred, and clear. These different patterns can occur anywhere in the muskie's range.

BARRED MUSKIE — Sides with wide, dark vertical bars on a lighter background.

CLEAR MUSKIE — Sides light brownish or greenish with no spots or bars.

Hybrids — Hybridizes naturally with northern pike, producing the tiger muskie. Many fish hatcheries also produce tiger muskies.

TIGER MUSKIE — Sides with irregular, narrow, vertical bars on lighter background; often, bars are broken into spots. Tips of tail rounder than those of purebred muskie.

Table Quality — The white, flaky meat is good eating, but the modern trend is toward catch-and-release because of the muskie's sport value.

Sporting Qualities — The muskie's moody, unpredictable nature has fascinated generations of anglers. Muskie fishing becomes an obsession for many, even though they catch very few. Muskie fishermen commonly use foot-long plugs and spinners, and baitfish weighing over a pound. They use stout baitcasting rods and 30- to 50-pound dacron line, always with a wire leader. Hooked muskies wage a spectacular but usually short battle. They leap and make powerful runs that often break the line or straighten the hook.

Habitat — Generally found in shallow weedy portions of natural lakes, or in slow-moving, weedy rivers. Cabbage weed makes ideal muskie cover, and in some areas is referred to as "lungeweed." Muskies do not thrive in lakes with heavy northern pike populations; northerns hatch earlier and eat the smaller muskie fry.

Big muskies prefer much warmer water than big northerns. They are normally found in water from 67° to 72°F, but will tolerate water up to 80°.

Food Habits — Fish are the muskie's favorite food. But like northerns, they eat whatever they can find, including frogs, crayfish, mice, muskrats and ducklings. Muskies prefer large food items, and where large foods are not available, their growth is slow.

Spawning Habits — Spawn in mid- to late spring, later than northern pike. The water temperature at spawning time varies from 49° to 59°F. Muskies pair off at spawning time, and it is common to see a big female cruising the shoreline accompanied by one or two smaller males. The eggs are scattered at random, usually over vegetation. The parents do not guard the young.

Age and Growth — Muskies grow more rapidly than other members of the pike family. They have been known to live over 30 years. Females grow faster and live longer than males.

Typical Length (inches) at Various Ages

Age	1	3	5	7	9	11	13	15	17
North	10.5	21.4	30.3	36.3	41.0	44.2	47.3	49.9	51.9
South	11.6	26.9	35.2	40.8	44.6	48.0	50.6	—	—

Typical Weight (pounds) at Various Lengths (inches)

Length	20	25	30	35	40	45	50	55
Weight	1.4	3.3	5.9	11.9	18.0	23.8	31.9	46.0

World Record — 69 pounds, 15 ounces, caught in the St. Lawrence River, New York, in 1957. A 102-pound muskie is said to have been netted from Lake Superior in the early 1900s, but the report has never been authenticated.

40-inch spotted muskie — Wolf Lake, Minnesota

Chain Pickerel *(Esox niger)*

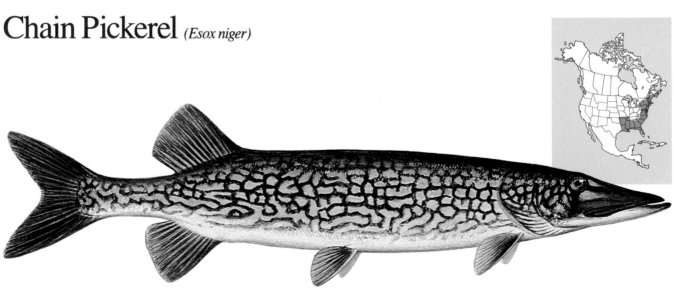

Common Names — Pike, river pike, grass pike, jack, jackfish, eastern pickerel.

Description — The chain pickerel gets its name from the dark chain-link markings on the side. The

3-pound chain pickerel — Orange Lake, Florida

background varies from green to bronze. The underside of the lower jaw has 8 pores. The cheek and gill cover are completely scaled (see photo above).

Hybrids — Known to hybridize with redfin pickerel and northern pike.

Table Quality — The white, flaky meat is good-tasting, but quite bony.

Sporting Qualities — Chain pickerel are much more popular than redfin pickerel because they grow considerably larger and are strong, acrobatic fighters. Productive lures include streamers, spinners, weedless spoons, surface plugs, crankbaits and jigs. Minnows are a reliable year-round bait, and account for most of the chain pickerel caught by ice fishermen.

Habitat — Normally found in clear, quiet waters with heavy weed growth. In warmwater streams, they inhabit areas with little or no current. They prefer water temperatures from 75° to 80°F.

Food Habits — The chain pickerel's diet is mainly fish. They also eat insects, frogs, mice, crayfish and a wide variety of other foods.

Spawning Habits — Spawn in spring, generally at a water temperature of about 45°F. The eggs are scattered over vegetation in shallow bays of lakes or in still areas of streams. The parents do not guard the eggs or fry.

Age and Growth — The maximum age is about 10 years. Females grow faster than males.

Typical Length (inches) at Various Ages

Age	1	2	3	4	5	6	7	8
Length	7.1	10.2	13.3	16.1	18.2	20.1	21.8	22.7

Typical Weight (pounds) at Various Lengths (inches)

Length	16	18	20	22	24	26	28
Weight	.90	1.2	1.7	2.3	3.4	5.6	7.9

World Record — 9 pounds, 6 ounces, caught in Guest Millpond, Georgia, in 1961.

Redfin Pickerel *(Esox americanus)*

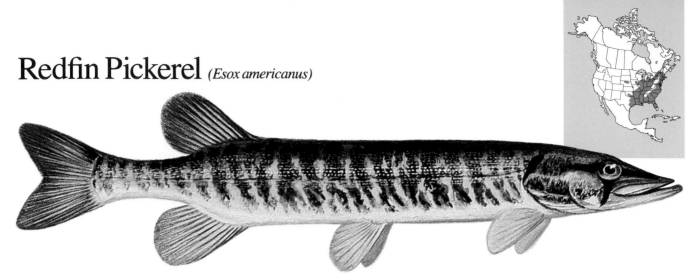

REDFIN PICKEREL — Pale areas between vertical bands narrower than bands. Lower fins amber to reddish orange.

Dark bar below eye is slightly off vertical and usually curves toward the rear. Found along the Atlantic coast.

Common Names — Little pickerel, mud pickerel, grass pickerel, banded pickerel, redfinned pike.

Description — The sides are light brown to olive-green with 20 or more dark, wavy bars. There is a distinct dark, vertical bar below the eye. The snout is shorter than that of a chain pickerel. Normally there are 8 pores on the underside of the lower jaw. The cheek and gill cover are completely scaled (see photo below).

Subspecies — Two are recognized: the redfin pickerel *(Esox americanus americanus)*, and the mud or grass pickerel *(Esox americanus vermiculatus)*. This

nomenclature causes some confusion because one of the subspecies has the same name as the species.

GRASS PICKEREL — Pale areas between vertical bands wider than bands. Lower fins dusky to yellowish green. Dark bar below eye is nearly vertical and usually straight. Found mainly in Mississippi River drainage.

Hybrids — Both subspecies hybridize with chain pickerel and northern pike.

Table Quality — White, flaky, sweet-tasting meat, but quite bony.

Sporting Qualities — These pickerel are scrappy fighters, but their small size limits their popularity as sport fish. They can be caught on minnows, streamers, small spinners, spoons and plugs.

Habitat — Usually found in sluggish, weedy streams, in shallow, weedy bays of lakes or in weedy ponds. They prefer water from 75° to 80°F.

Food Habits — Small fish make up most of the diet, but they also eat aquatic insects and various other invertebrates.

Spawning Habits — Spawn in spring, usually at water temperatures of 48° to 52°F. Most spawning takes place along grassy stream banks, or in flooded backwaters. The eggs are scattered over vegetation, then abandoned.

Age and Growth — This species grows much more slowly than other members of the pike family. The maximum age is about 8 years, but the usual life span is 5 years or less. There is little difference in growth between males and females, although females live longer. Redfins generally grow faster than grass pickerel.

Typical Length (inches) at Various Ages

Age	1	2	3	4	5	6	7
Redfin	4.7	5.8	7.8	8.8	10.3	11.9	—
Grass	4.3	5.8	7.1	7.7	8.6	9.8	10.8

Typical Weight (pounds) at Various Lengths (inches)

Length	9	10	11	12	13	14	15	16	17
Weight	.14	.19	.26	.35	.45	.57	.71	.88	1.1

World Record — 1 pound, 8 ounces, caught in Bluff Lake, South Carolina, in 1984.

Grass pickerel — Big Darby Creek, Ohio

Perch Family

The tremendous popularity of this family of fish results mainly from their outstanding table quality. But the larger members of the family are excellent sport fish as well.

In Canada and some areas of the Great Lakes, these fish are harvested commercially and command a high price. But commercial fishing has been banned elsewhere because the sporting value of the fish far exceeds their commercial value.

Members of the perch family (*Percidae*) can be recognized by their long, cylindrical body and two dorsal fins. This widespread family consists of three groups: pike-perch, yellow perch and darters. Pike-perch include the walleye and sauger, which are the largest members of the family and are easily distin-guished by their prominent teeth and glassy eyes. Yellow perch are considerably smaller and do not have noticeable teeth or glassy eyes. Darters include more than 100 species, all too small to be caught by fishermen.

Pike-perch and yellow perch are considered cool-water fish. They require cold water temperatures for several months of the year. Otherwise, the repro-ductive organs do not mature. Consequently, these fish are not found in the Deep South, unless popula-tions are maintained by stocking.

Historically, pike-perch and yellow perch were not found west of the Rockies, but widespread stocking has established walleye and yellow perch popula-tions in most western states. Saugers have not been stocked as widely.

Walleyes, saugers and yellow perch are spring spawn-ers, capable of spawning in lakes or streams. They do not build nests, but scatter their eggs at random. The parents make no attempt to protect the eggs or the young.

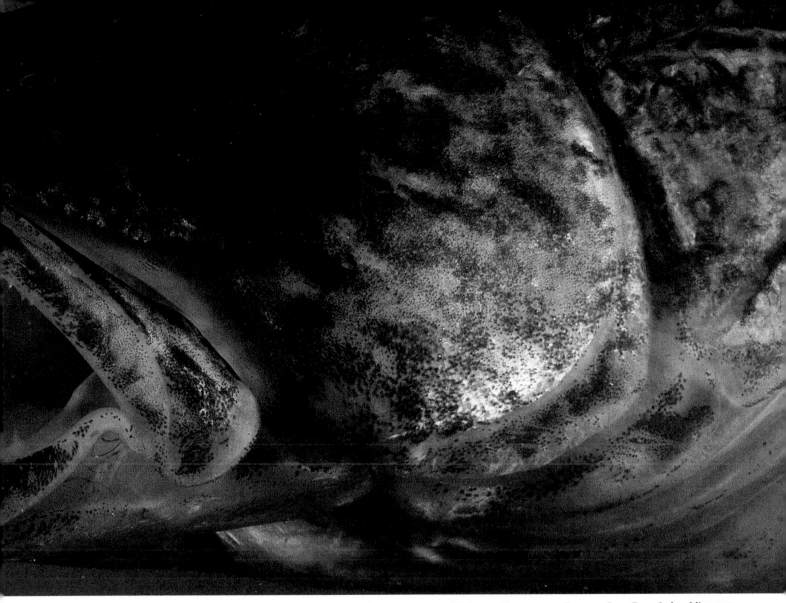

Walleye taking young yellow perch — Deer Lake, Minnesota

Perch Family — Species Identification Key

1 No fang-like teeth . . . . YELLOW PERCH

Large fang-like teeth . . . . go to 2

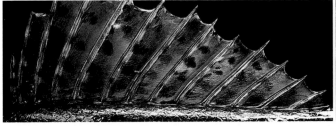

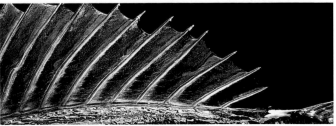

2 Several rows of dark spots on spiny dorsal fin . . . .
SAUGER

No rows of spots on spiny dorsal; rear of fin dark . . . .
WALLEYE

Yellow Perch *(Perca flavescens)*

Common Names — Raccoon perch, ringed perch, lake perch, redfin perch.

Description — The yellowish sides have 6 to 9 dark vertical bars. The lower fins are amber to bright orange. Females are not as brightly colored as males.

Eating Quality — One of the finest eating freshwater fish. The white, flaky meat is even firmer and tastier than that of walleye.

Sporting Qualities — Yellow perch are easy to catch, but are not strong fighters. Popular baits include small minnows, worms, leeches, crickets, grubs and crayfish tails. The most effective lures are small jigs and spinners.

Habitat — The largest yellow perch are found in open-water areas of large lakes with fairly clear water, a firm bottom and sparse to moderate vegetation. Small lakes, ponds and rivers usually produce smaller perch. Yellow perch prefer water temperatures from 65° to 72°F.

Food Habits — Important foods include immature aquatic insects, crayfish, snails, small fish and fish eggs. Perch feed most heavily during daylight hours.

Spawning Habits — Spawn in spring, normally at water temperatures from 43° to 48°F. Gelatinous strings of eggs are deposited over weeds or brush in the shallows of lakes or in tributary streams. Most spawning takes place at night or in early morning. Parents do not guard the eggs or fry.

Age and Growth — Maximum age is about 10 years. Growth is highly variable, depending upon the habitat.

Typical Length (inches) at Various Ages

Age	1	2	3	4	5	6	7	8	9
Length	3.0	4.9	6.7	8.1	9.3	10.0	10.6	11.0	11.2

Typical Weight (pounds) at Various Lengths (inches)

Length	7	8	9	10	11	12
Weight	.22	.29	.40	.57	.81	1.2

World Record — 4 pounds, 3 ounces, caught in the Delaware River, New Jersey, in 1865.

10- to 12-inch yellow perch — Ottertail Lake, Minnesota

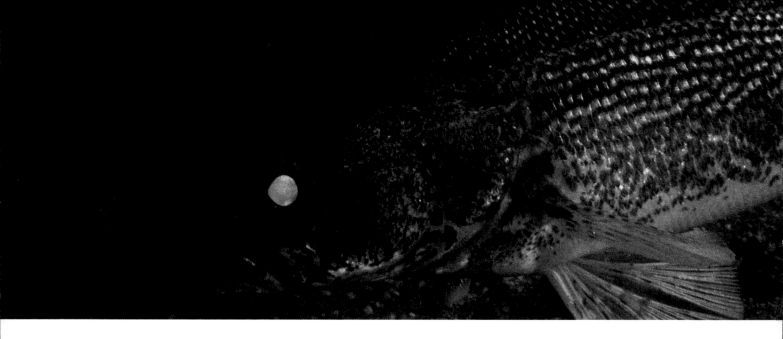

Sauger *(Stizostedion canadense)*

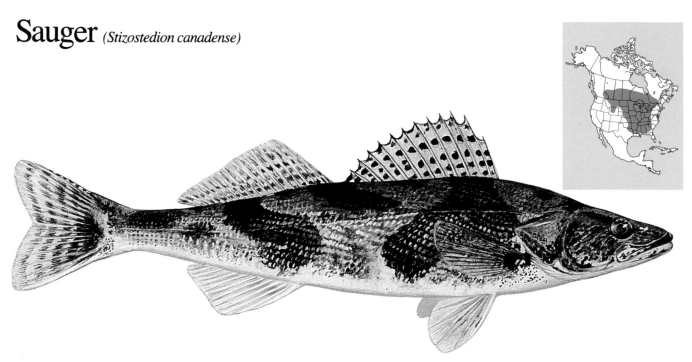

Common Names — Sand pike, river pike, gray pike, gray pickerel, spotfin pike.

Description — Sides are yellowish brown to gray with darker brown blotches. The spiny dorsal fin has several rows of distinct black spots. There is a black spot at the base of the pectoral fin. The tail may have a thin, white lower margin, but there is no white corner as on the walleye. The eyes have a silvery sheen and reflect light.

20-inch sauger — St. Croix River, Wisconsin

Hybrids — Sauger often hybridizes with walleye to produce the *saugeye*.

SAUGEYE — Spots on spiny dorsal fin not as round as those of sauger. Sides may have faint blotches and a gold cast. White streak on lower edge of tail, but no white corner.

Table Quality — Excellent; the white, flaky meat is identical to that of a walleye.

Sporting Qualities — Saugers are usually caught by trolling or drifting with minnows, nightcrawlers or leeches. The best lures are jigs, deep-running plugs and vibrating blades. Like walleyes, saugers wage a strong battle in deep water.

Habitat — The eyes of a sauger are even more light-sensitive than those of a walleye, so saugers are normally found in deeper water. The best sauger populations occur in big, slow-moving, muddy rivers, or large, shallow lakes with murky water. Saugers prefer water temperatures from 62° to 72°F.

Food Habits — The diet consists mainly of fish, but saugers also eat aquatic insect larvae, leeches and crayfish. Their excellent night vision enables them to find food easily after dark or in deep water.

Spawning Habits — Spawn in spring, normally at water temperatures of 47° to 52°F. In rivers, saugers usually migrate upstream to a dam or other barrier, then deposit their eggs over a sand or gravel bottom where there is light current. In lakes, the eggs are deposited on gravel or rubble shoals. Most spawning takes place at night. The parents do not protect the eggs or fry.

Age and Growth — Saugers grow more slowly and are shorter-lived than walleyes. The maximum age is about 13 years.

Typical Length (inches) at Various Ages

Age	1	2	3	4	5	6	7
North	5.6	9.2	12.1	14.3	16.0	17.2	17.8
South	7.4	13.1	15.6	18.0	18.7	19.6	20.3

Typical Weight (pounds) at Various Lengths (inches)

Length	10	12	14	16	18	20
Weight	.36	.62	.98	1.5	2.0	2.6

World Record — 8 pounds, 12 ounces, caught in Lake Sakakawea, North Dakota, in 1971.

Walleye *(Stizostedion vitreum)*

Common Names — Walleyed pike, pickerel, jackfish and doré.

Description — The sides are olive-green with gold flecks. The spiny dorsal fin lacks spots, but has a black rear base. The lower lobe of the tail has a white tip.

Subspecies — At one time, there were two subspecies: the yellow walleye *(Stizostedion vitreum vitreum)* and the blue walleye or blue pike *(Stizostedion vitreum glaucum)*. The blue walleye was common in lakes Erie and Ontario, but is now thought to be extinct.

Hybrids — Commonly hybridizes with the sauger to produce the saugeye (page 107).

Table Quality — Walleyes are considered one of the finest table fish. The white, flaky meat has a very mild flavor.

Sporting Qualities — Strong fighters, walleyes stay deep and wage a determined battle. Because of their light-sensitive eyes, they bite best around dusk and dawn, at night, or in cloudy weather. Popular baits and lures include minnows, nightcrawlers, leeches, jigs, spinners and plugs, especially minnow plugs.

Habitat — Most numerous in large, windswept natural lakes of moderate to low clarity. They can also be found in smaller lakes, reservoirs, and rivers and streams with moderate current. Walleyes prefer clean, hard bottoms and water temperatures from 65° to 75°F.

Food Habits — Primarily fish eaters, walleyes also feed on immature and adult aquatic insects, leeches, crayfish, snails and larval salamanders. Except in waters of low clarity, they feed most heavily in dim-light periods, especially when light levels are fading rapidly.

Spawning Habits — Spawn in spring, usually along a shallow, windswept shoreline with a rubble bottom. The water temperature at spawning time is normally 45° to 50°F. The eggs are broadcast at random, and the parents do not attempt to guard the eggs or fry.

Age and Growth — Walleyes have been known to live as long as 26 years. Females typically grow much larger than males.

Typical Length (inches) at Various Ages

Age	1	2	3	4	5	7	9	11	13
North	6.0	9.8	12.1	14.0	15.5	17.8	20.0	23.0	25.3
South	9.3	15.1	18.7	21.3	23.5	27.2	29.7	—	—

Typical Weight (pounds) at Various Lengths (inches)

Length	12	14	16	18	20	22	24	26	28	30
Weight	.65	1.0	1.5	2.0	2.8	3.8	4.9	6.3	8.0	10.0

World Record — 25 pounds, caught in Old Hickory Lake, Tennessee, in 1960.

3- to 4-pound walleyes — Round Lake, Wisconsin

35-pound flathead catfish — St. Croix River, Minnesota/Wisconsin border

Catfish Family

Catfish Family

Many anglers would be surprised to learn that catfish and bullheads rank among the country's most popular sportfish. Only bass and panfish have a larger following of freshwater fishermen.

This tremendous popularity is easy to understand. A big cat is as strong a fighter as any freshwater fish; and fried catfish or bullhead is difficult to beat on the dinner table.

Members of the catfish family (*Ictaluridae*) of greatest interest to anglers include four species of catfish and three species of bullheads. The family also includes *madtoms,* but these catfish are too small to catch on hook and line.

Historically, none of these species were found west of the Rocky Mountains. Because of widespread stocking, however, catfish or bullheads are found in practically every state.

Members of the catfish family are easy to recognize. They have four pairs of barbels, or whiskers. They have an adipose fin on the rear of the back, similar to the adipose fin of a trout. And they have smooth, tough skin that lacks scales.

The easiest way to distinguish catfish from bullheads is the shape of the tail. All catfish, with the exception of flatheads, have forked tails. The tails of bullheads are square or rounded.

Although catfish and bullheads have poor eyesight, the barbels are well-equipped with taste buds, making it possible for them to find food at night or in muddy water.

Other special adaptations include the sharp spines on the dorsal and pectoral fins, and the bands of small, recurved teeth on the roof of mouth. The spines can inflict a painful wound, discouraging predators. The bands of recurved teeth make it almost impossible for prey to escape once a catfish or bullhead grabs it.

Like sunfish, members of the catfish family are nest builders. One or both of the parents excavate the nest, usually in a dimly lit area near heavy cover. Males guard the nest and protect the fry for several days after they hatch.

Catfish and bullheads are *omnivores,* meaning that they will eat practically any type of food. Consequently, anglers use an unbelievable variety of baits from sun-ripened chicken livers to *stink baits* to 2-pound carp. The most productive fishing technique is still-fishing on bottom, waiting for the scent to attract the fish.

Because of their table quality, catfish bring a high price on the commercial market. As a result, trotliners and other commercial fishermen have overharvested catfish populations in some areas. The effects are most noticeable on the larger fish. Some progressive natural-resources agencies have taken steps to limit commercial fishing, resulting in higher quality fishing for anglers.

Catfish Family — Species Identification Key

1 *Tail deeply forked* . . . . *go to* **2**   *Tail rounded or square* . . . . *go to* **3**

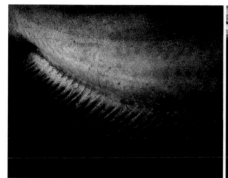

2 Anal fin with 30 or more rays . . . . .   Anal fin with 24 to 29 rays . . . .   Anal fin with 19 to 23 rays . . . .
 BLUE CATFISH   CHANNEL CATFISH   WHITE CATFISH

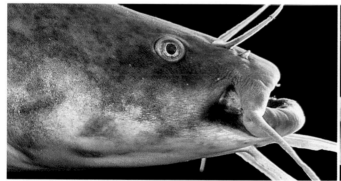

3 Lower jaw projecting beyond upper . . . .   *Upper jaw projecting beyond lower* . . . . *go to* **4**
 FLATHEAD CATFISH

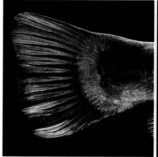

4 Chin barbels whitish . . .   *Chin barbels grayish or*   **5** Light, crescent-shaped   No light, crescent-shaped
 YELLOW BULLHEAD   *blackish* . . . . *go to* **5**   mark at base of tail . . . .   mark at base of tail . . . . . .
     BLACK BULLHEAD   BROWN BULLHEAD

Blue Catfish *(Ictalurus furcatus)*

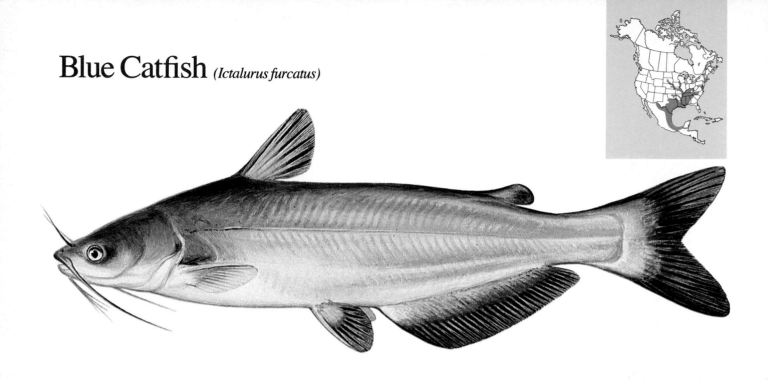

Common Names — Forktail cat, great blue cat, chucklehead cat, silver cat, blue fulton.

Description — Closely resembles the channel catfish. The tail is deeply forked, but the bluish to grayish sides are unspotted, even on young fish. The anal fin is longer than that of a channel cat and has a straighter edge.

Hybrids — Known to hybridize with channel catfish.

Table Quality — Considered an excellent food fish with a fine, delicate flavor.

Sporting Qualities — One of the strongest freshwater gamefish, blue catfish are caught by trotlining, jug fishing and *noodling* (grabbing by hand), as well as angling. The most effective baits are cut fish, live fish and nightcrawlers. Blue cats will also take prepared and rotting baits.

Habitat — Blue catfish occur naturally in big rivers and the lower reaches of their major tributaries. They have been stocked in many reservoirs and ponds. They prefer clearer, swifter water than other catfish, and are usually found over a sand, gravel or rock bottom. Their preferred water temperature is 77° to 82°F.

Food Habits — Blue cats feed most heavily at night, but they do some feeding during the day. Their diet consists mainly of fish, immature aquatic insects, crayfish and clams. A big blue cat can eat a fish weighing several pounds.

Spawning Habits — Spawn in late spring and summer, usually at water temperatures of 70° to 75°F. Males build nests under logs or brush, or in holes in the riverbank. After spawning, males remain on guard until the fry leave the nest.

Age and Growth — Blue catfish up to 14 years old have been recorded, but they undoubtedly live much longer. Females grow slightly faster than males.

Typical Length (inches) at Various Ages

Age	1	2	3	4	5	6	7	8	9	10
Length	6.2	11.1	14.7	18.3	22.1	25.5	28.8	30.6	32.3	34.1

Typical Weight (pounds) at Various Lengths (inches)

Length	20	24	28	32	36	40	44	48
Weight	2.9	5.4	9.5	15.3	23.2	33.7	47.3	64.4

World Record — 97 pounds, caught in the Missouri River, South Dakota, in 1959. Many blue cats exceeding 100 pounds have been caught, but never officially recorded.

52-pound blue catfish — Lake Hamilton, Arkansas

Channel Catfish *(Ictalurus punctatus)*

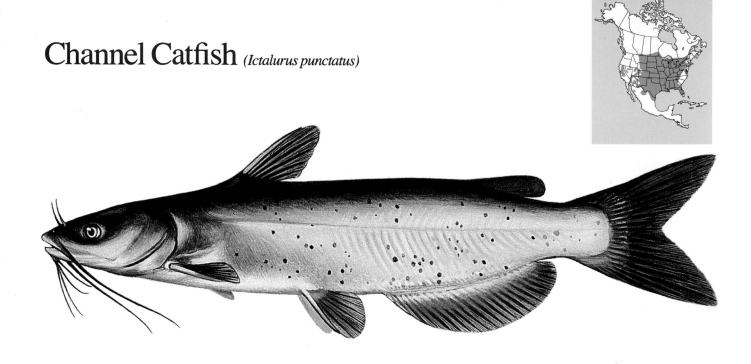

Common Names — Spotted cat, blue channel cat, Great Lakes catfish and lady cat. Young channel cats are called fiddlers.

Description — Sides vary from dark bluish gray to greenish gray to silver, usually with dark spots, although large individuals may be unspotted. The tail is deeply forked; the anal fin is shorter than that of the blue cat and its edge is more rounded.

Hybrids — On rare occasion, hybridizes with blue and flathead cats.

Table Quality — Considered one of the best-eating freshwater fish. The meat is white, tender and sweet when the fish is taken from clean water. Any off-taste can usually be eliminated by discarding the reddish meat from the sides.

Sporting Qualities — Most channel cats are caught by bottom fishing with baits ranging from dried chicken blood to nightcrawlers to pieces of soap. They prefer dead or prepared baits to live bait, but at times will take live minnows and lures such as spinners and jigs. Channel cats are strong fighters with remarkable endurance.

Habitat — Most common in big rivers, especially in deep stretches with sand, gravel or rubble bottoms. They like some current, but not as much as blue catfish. Channels are also found in lakes, reservoirs and ponds. Their preferred temperature range is 75° to 80°F.

Food Habits — Feed both at night and during the day on aquatic insect larvae, clams, snails, crayfish, crabs, fish and aquatic plants.

Spawning Habits — Spawn in late spring or summer, normally at water temperatures from 70° to 75°F. Males build nests under logs, in the shade of boulders, in holes in the bank, in barrels, or in other dark, secluded spots. Males guard the nest until the fry leave.

Age and Growth — There have been records of channel cats reaching 40 years of age. They grow faster than white catfish, but slower than blues or flatheads.

Typical Length (inches) at Various Ages

Age	1	2	3	4	5	6	7	8	9
North	5.7	7.1	9.0	10.5	12.3	14.1	15.9	18.4	19.7
South	10.9	13.7	15.7	17.8	19.0	21.6	22.6	23.5	24.3

Typical Weight (pounds) at Various Lengths (inches)

Length	12	15	18	21	24	27	30	33	36
Weight	.5	1.3	2.7	3.3	5.8	8.8	11.6	15.3	20.4

World Record — 58 pounds, caught in the Santee-Cooper Reservoir, South Carolina, in 1964.

14-pound channel catfish — Chippewa River, Wisconsin

White Catfish *(Ictalurus catus)*

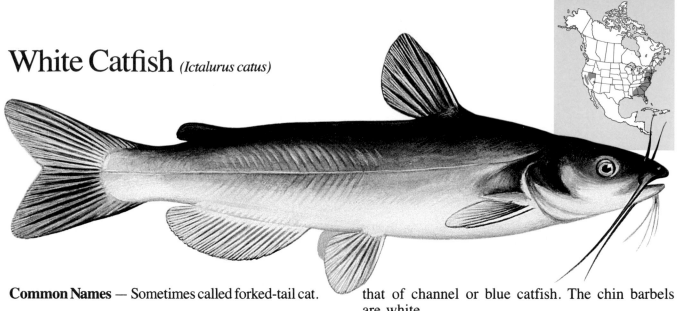

Common Names — Sometimes called forked-tail cat.

Description — The sides are gray-blue to blue-black and may be mottled. The tail is moderately forked, and the anal fin is shorter and rounder than that of channel or blue catfish. The chin barbels are white.

Table Quality — The firm, white meat makes this catfish an excellent food fish.

Sporting Qualities — Willing biters, white catfish are often used for stocking pay-as-you-go fishing ponds. Although they are good fighters, they have not become as popular as channel catfish because of their considerably smaller size. Live bait, especially minnows and worms, accounts for most white catfish, but they will also take cut baits and prepared baits.

Habitat — Usually found in slow-moving streams, river backwaters, reservoirs and ponds. They prefer slower-moving water than channel or blue catfish, and will tolerate a siltier bottom and higher salinity. They prefer water temperatures of 80° to 85°F.

Food Habits — Fish are the major food item, but white catfish also eat larval aquatic insects, small crustaceans, fish eggs, aquatic plants and plant seeds. They may feed at night, but are not as nocturnal as other catfish.

Spawning Habits — Spawn in late spring or early summer, usually at water temperatures from 70° to 75°F. Both parents help excavate the large nest, usually on a sand or gravel bar. The eggs and fry are guarded by one or both parents.

Age and Growth — White catfish grow more slowly than other catfish species. They have been known to live as long as 14 years.

Typical Length (inches) at Various Ages

Age	1	2	3	4	5	6	8	10	12
North	4.6	5.9	7.3	8.3	9.6	10.4	13.3	16.7	20.0
South	4.9	6.6	9.5	12.2	14.9	16.3	18.9	—	—

Typical Weight (pounds) at Various Lengths (inches)

Length	8	10	12	14	16	18	20	22
Weight	.17	.35	.64	1.0	1.7	2.3	3.2	4.3

World Record — 17 pounds, 7 ounces, caught in Success Lake, California, in 1981.

2-pound white catfish — Lake Lanier, Georgia

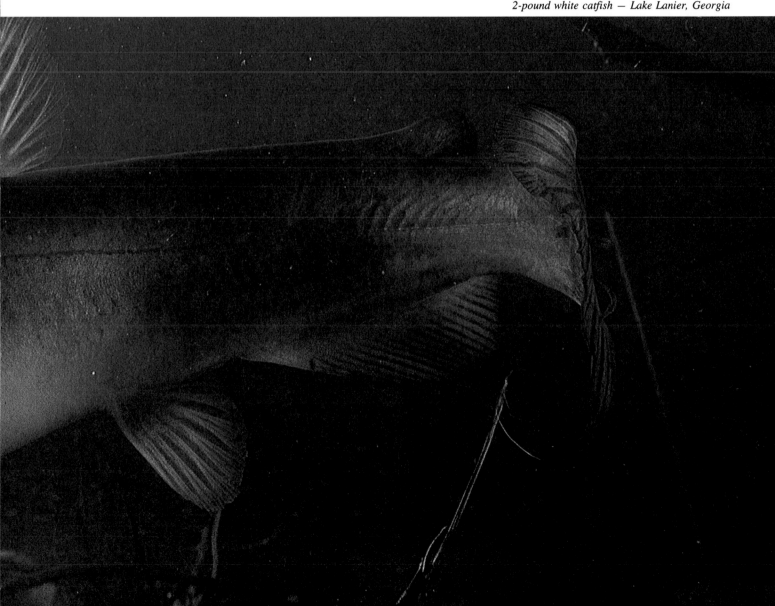

Flathead Catfish *(Pylodictis olivaris)*

Common Names — Mud cat, yellow cat, shovelhead cat, johnnie cat, goujon, appaluchion.

Description — Sides are brownish yellow and usually mottled. The flattened head, tiny eyes, squarish tail and protruding lower jaw give the flathead a much different appearance than other catfish. Small flatheads may be confused with bullheads, but the tooth pad on the upper jaw of a flathead has backward extensions on each end (photo at right).

Hybrids — Known to hybridize with channel catfish.

Table Quality — The meat is white, firm, flaky and good-tasting in fish taken from clean water.

Sporting Qualities — Extremely strong fighters, but their solitary lifestyle makes them more difficult to catch than other catfish. They often mouth the bait several times before swallowing it, causing fishermen to set the hook too soon. Flatheads bite best at night, combing the shallows in search of food. During the day, they lie in heavy cover. More are probably taken by trotlining, jug fishing and noodling (page 115) than by angling. Live fish are considered the best bait, but some flatheads are caught on cut pieces of fresh fish, and on crayfish and nightcrawlers. Unlike channel and blue cats, they are reluctant to take prepared or rotting baits.

Habitat — Found mainly in large rivers and their major tributaries, and in reservoirs. In rivers, they prefer long, deep, sluggish pools with hard bottoms, and often lie in a tangle of submerged logs. Their preferred temperature range is 78° to 82°F.

Food Habits — Fish, crayfish and clams make up most of the flathead's diet.

Spawning Habits — Spawn in late spring or early summer, normally at temperatures of 70° to 80°F. One or both parents excavate the nest, which is usually in a natural cavity like a hole in the bank, or near a log or some other large, submerged object. After spawning, the male guards the nest until the fry disperse.

Age and Growth — The maximum documented age is 19 years, but they probably live much longer. They grow faster than other catfish, with the exception of blues.

Typical Length (inches) at Various Ages

Age	1	2	3	5	7	9	11	13	15
North	7.5	10.9	14.8	19.3	23.9	28.0	35.5	37.0	40.0
South	—	16.3	24.3	27.7	34.7	36.3	40.4	44.2	46.3

Typical Weight (pounds) at Various Lengths (inches)

Length	20	25	30	35	40	45	50
Weight	3.4	6.7	12.1	20.0	30.2	51.3	70.2

World Record — 98 pounds, caught near the floodgate on Lake Lewisville, Texas, in 1986. Many flatheads over 100 pounds have been reported, but never officially recognized.

Flathead catfish among submerged branches — Mississippi River, Wisconsin

Yellow Bullhead *(Ictalurus natalis)*

Common Names — Yellow cat, creek cat, white-whiskered bullhead and greaser.

Description — The sides are yellow to yellow-brown with no mottling. The chin barbels are yellow

Male yellow bullhead guarding fry — Clear Lake, Iowa

to buff to pale pink; the upper barbels, light to dark brown. The anal fin has a straight margin; the tail is rounded.

Table Quality — The cream-colored meat has a good flavor, but tends to become soft in summer.

Sporting Qualities — Easy to catch on cut bait, worms, crickets, doughballs and a wide variety of other natural and prepared baits. They can be caught at any time of day, but bite best at night. They are not strong fighters.

Habitat — Yellow bullheads prefer clear, heavily vegetated waters, but are more tolerant of polluted water and low oxygen levels than other bullhead species. They are found in small, shallow lakes; shallow bays of larger lakes; ponds; and sluggish warmwater streams. They prefer water temperatures from 75° to 80°F.

Food Habits — Primarily scavengers, yellow bullheads eat bits of aquatic vegetation, crustaceans, immature aquatic insects, snails, and occasionally live fish.

Spawning Habits — Spawn in late spring or early summer, usually at water temperatures in the upper 60s or low 70s. One or both parents build the nest, which may be a shallow depression in an open area or a deep burrow in the bank. After spawning, the male guards the eggs and fry.

Age and Growth — Yellow bullheads live up to 7 years. They seldom reach the dense population levels common with black bullheads, so they are less likely to become stunted.

Typical Length (inches) at Various Ages

Age	1	2	3	4	5
North	2.1	5.1	9.3	10.9	12.7
South	2.9	7.2	11.2	12.9	15.3

Typical Weight (pounds) at Various Lengths (inches)

Length	6	8	10	12	14	16	18
Weight	.18	.26	.50	.87	1.4	2.1	3.0

World Record — 4 pounds, 4 ounces, caught in Mormon Lake, Arizona, in 1984. Illinois lists a 5-pound, 4-ounce yellow bullhead caught in 1954.

Brown Bullhead *(Ictalurus nebulosus)*

NORTHERN BROWN BULLHEAD — Mottling on sides vague compared to that of southern brown bullhead. Found in the northern two-thirds of the brown bullhead range; widely stocked in the West.

Common Names — Horned pout, mud cat, creek cat, and red cat. The latter refers to the reddish color of the flesh.

Description — Sides are yellowish to brownish and normally mottled. The whiskers are dark brown to black. The tail is square or slightly notched. The anal fin has a rounded edge. The barbs on the pectoral spine (photo at right) are longer than those of a black bullhead. See subspecies descriptions.

Subspecies — Two are recognized: the northern brown bullhead *(Ictalurus nebulosus nebulosus)* and the southern brown bullhead *(Ictalurus nebulosus marmoratus)*.

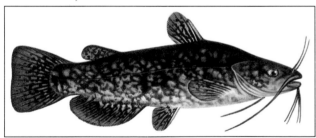

SOUTHERN BROWN BULLHEAD — Distinct brownish mottling over a light background. Found in the southern one-third of the brown bullhead range.

Hybrids — Known to hybridize with black bullhead.

Table Quality — The reddish to pinkish meat is firm and has an excellent flavor.

Sporting Qualities — Fair fighters, brown bullheads are easy to catch on baits such as worms, minnows, shrimp, chicken innards and stinkbait.

They bite throughout the day, but fishing is best at night.

Habitat — Inhabit larger, deeper lakes than other bullheads, but are also found in warmwater ponds, smaller lakes and sluggish streams. They prefer water temperatures of 78° to 82°F, but can survive at temperatures up to 97°.

Food Habits — Brown bullheads eat a wide variety of foods, including aquatic plants and algae, small fish, fish eggs, insects, snails, crayfish, worms and leeches.

Spawning Habits — Spawn in late spring or early summer, at water temperatures from 70° to 75°F. Both parents construct the nest on a mud or sand bottom, often among plant roots or other cover that offers shade. After spawning, one or both parents guard the nest. They continue to protect the young for several weeks after hatching.

Age and Growth — The maximum age is about 12 years. Brown bullheads in the South grow considerably faster than those in the North.

Typical Length (inches) at Various Ages

Age	1	2	3	4	5	6
North	5.0	7.3	8.7	10.3	11.0	11.4
South	3.6	7.1	10.2	12.3	14.2	—

Typical Weight (pounds) at Various Lengths (inches)

Length	8	10	12	14	16	18	20
Weight	.26	.53	.90	1.5	2.1	3.1	4.2

World Record — 5 pounds, 8 ounces, caught in Veal Pond, Georgia, in 1975. Minnesota lists a 7-pound, 1-ounce brown bullhead caught in Shallow Lake in 1974.

Northern brown bullheads — Long Lake, Minnesota

Black Bullhead *(Ictalurus melas)*

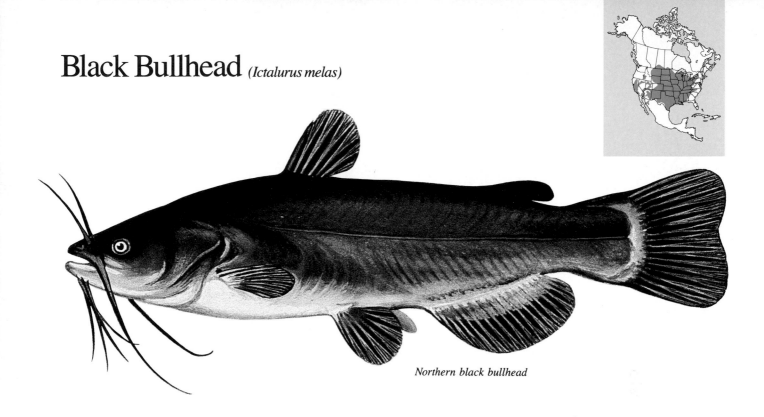

Northern black bullhead

Common Names — Horned pout, yellowbelly bullhead, black catfish.

Description — Sides are green to gold, with a lustrous sheen and no mottling. The barbels are gray or black. The tail is slightly notched, usually with a pale bar at the base; the anal fin is rounded, with a gray base. The pectoral spines are weakly barbed (photo at right) and may be almost smooth on older fish; the spines of a brown bullhead have strong barbs.

Subspecies — Two are recognized: the northern black bullhead *(Ictalurus melas melas)*, found in the northern states and Canada; and the southern black bullhead *(Ictalurus melas catulus)*, found in the southern states and northern Mexico. The main difference is the longer pectoral spine in the southern subspecies.

Hybrids — Known to hybridize with brown bullhead.

Table Quality — The meat is white and has a good flavor, but may be soft in summer.

Sporting Qualities — Not strong fighters. They tend to spin when reeled in. Worms are the most popular bait, but they will take many others like cheese, doughballs, stinkbaits and liver.

Habitat — Most numerous in streams and lakes with murky water, soft bottoms and no noticeable current. Black bullheads can tolerate pollution and low levels of dissolved oxygen, and often are the only fish found in freeze-out lakes. They prefer water temperatures from 75° to 85°F.

Food Habits — Black bullheads will eat almost anything including clams, snails, small fish, fish eggs, insects, and plant material.

Spawning Habits — Spawn in late spring or summer, usually at water temperatures from 66° to 70°F. The female prepares the nest, usually in a weedy area or beneath woody cover. When spawning is completed, she helps the male guard the eggs and fry. After the fry leave the nest, they are often seen swimming about in tight schools.

Age and Growth — Because of their high reproductive rate, black bullheads tend to become overpopulated, resulting in slow growth. The maximum life span is about 10 years, although few survive past age 5.

Typical Length (inches) at Various Ages

Age	1	2	3	4	5	6	7	8
North	5.3	6.5	8.1	8.9	9.6	11.3	11.8	12.1
South	3.7	6.7	9.0	10.8	12.3	13.8	—	—

Typical Weight (pounds) at Various Lengths (inches)

Length	6	8	10	12	14	16	18
Weight	.11	.27	.67	1.1	1.6	2.2	3.0

World Record — 8 pounds, caught in Lake Waccabuc, New York, in 1951.

Northern black bullheads — Langdon Lake, Minnesota

Sturgeon & Paddlefish Families

Some of these primitive fishes have existed in their present form for nearly 100 million years. Both sturgeon and paddlefish bear a strong resemblance to sharks. The spine extends through the elongated upper lobe of the tail, the skin does not have scales, and the skeleton consists of cartilage rather than bone. Sturgeon are easily recognized by the large, bony plates, or *scutes*, on the body and by the four barbels dangling from the snout. Paddlefish have a flat bill about one-third of their total length.

The sturgeon family *(Acipenseridae)* includes seven North American species. Of these, three live strictly in fresh water, and four are anadromous, living in the sea and swimming into fresh water to spawn. We will discuss only the three species of greatest importance to anglers.

The paddlefish family *(Polyodontidae)* has only two living species, one in North America and another in China.

Sturgeon are the largest fish in North American fresh waters. Along the Pacific Coast, white sturgeon have been known to reach weights of nearly a ton. Although sturgeon grow very slowly, they may live 80 years or more.

Fresh or smoked sturgeon and paddlefish are considered excellent eating, and the eggs are used to make caviar. Before the era of modern fish and game regulations, sturgeon were killed for their eggs and thousands of tons of meat left to rot on the beaches. Sturgeon were also killed to obtain *isinglass,* a gelatinous substance made from the lining of the swim bladder. Isinglass is used mainly for clarifying wine and beer.

Sturgeon and paddlefish numbers have declined drastically in most areas as a result of overharvest, pollution, and construction of dams which block spawning migrations. Once a population has been depleted, rebuilding it is very difficult because of the slow growth and late maturity of these fishes.

Lake sturgeon combing the bottom for food — St. Croix River, Minnesota

Sturgeon and Paddlefish Families — Species Identification Key

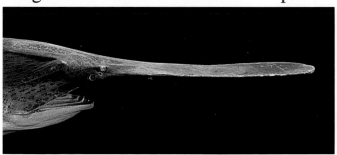

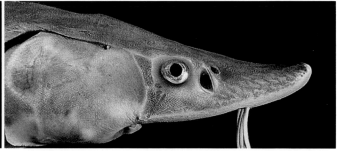

1 Long, paddle-like snout . . . . PADDLEFISH

Shorter snout . . . . *go to 2*

2 *Small opening, or spiracle (arrow), on gill cover* . . . *go to 3*

No small opening on gill cover . . . . SHOVELNOSE STURGEON

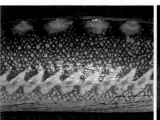
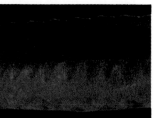

3 Sides usually with small white spots . . . . WHITE STURGEON

Sides plain, without small white spots . . . . LAKE STURGEON

Paddlefish *(Polyodon spathula)*

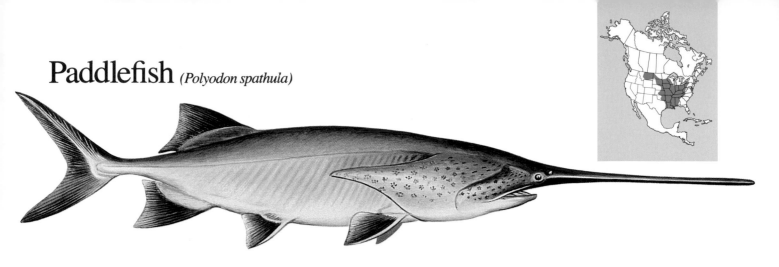

Paddlefish filtering plankton — Missouri River, South Dakota

Common Names — Spoonbill, spoonbill cat, shovelnose cat and spadefish.

Description — The long, flattened snout and the pointed gill cover extending to the middle of the body make it nearly impossible to mistake the paddlefish for any other species.

Table Quality — The firm, white meat is very good eating, either fresh or smoked. The eggs make excellent caviar. Some commercial caviar contains both sturgeon and paddlefish eggs.

Sporting Qualities — Paddlefish are strong fighters; their large size and the strong current in which they are usually found demand very heavy tackle. They rarely take a baited hook, but can be caught with snagging gear. Snag-fishermen use stout rods, heavy line with a big sinker at the end, and several treble hooks tied 1 to 3 feet apart.

Habitat — Most common in slow-moving stretches of large rivers and in adjoining backwaters, particularly where the bottom is muddy. Paddlefish can survive in reservoirs if they have access to a free-flowing section of river that meets their spawning requirements. They prefer relatively cool water, from 55° to 60°F, and stop feeding when the temperature exceeds 68°.

Food Habits — A paddlefish feeds by swimming about with its mouth open wide, filtering plankton from the water with its closely spaced gill rakers. As it feeds, the bill sways slowly from side to side. Contrary to popular belief, the bill is not used to root organisms from the bottom, but rather to feel for concentrations of plankton. The huge gill chamber enables paddlefish to filter enormous quantities of water. Fish occasionally are found in paddlefish stomachs, but probably were swallowed by accident.

Spawning Habits — Spawn in spring when the water level is rising, usually at temperatures of 50° to 60°F. The eggs are deposited randomly on silt-free gravel bars that were exposed to the air or barely submerged at normal water stage. The parents do not guard the eggs or fry.

Age and Growth — Paddlefish grow rapidly in their early years, then growth slows considerably. They reach ages of 30 years or more.

Typical Length (inches) at Various Ages

Age	1	3	5	7	9	12	15	18	21
North	8.1	27.2	36.0	48.0	53.3	55.9	62.4	62.8	64.2
South	19.1	35.8	53.2	61.0	64.9	67.7	—	—	—

Typical Weight (pounds) at Various Lengths (inches)

Length	34	40	46	52	58	64	70	76
Weight	5.7	9.7	14.5	23.6	29.2	40.4	55.2	67.5

World Record — No official record, but a 142-pound, 8-ounce paddlefish was caught in the Missouri River, Montana, in 1973.

Shovelnose Sturgeon *(Scaphirhynchus platorynchus)*

Common Names — Hackleback, switchtail, sand sturgeon, flathead sturgeon.

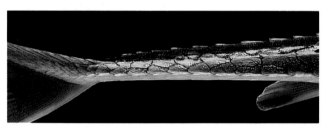

Description — Easily identified by the long, flattened snout; strongly fringed barbels; and extremely thin caudal peduncle covered with bony plates (photo above). A long filament extends off the upper lobe of the tail, although the filament is often broken off. There is no spiracle on the gill cover.

Table Quality — The firm, white meat is considered excellent eating, either fresh or smoked. The eggs make good caviar.

Sporting Qualities — Occasionally taken with rod and reel, but more often on setlines baited with cut fish, minnows or worms. Shovelnose sturgeon often jump when hooked, and put up a strong fight for their size.

Habitat — Usually found in the swift current of large rivers over a sand or gravel bottom, especially where there are concentrations of snails and clams. They can tolerate very murky water and prefer temperatures from 70° to 75°F.

Food Habits — The shovelnose sturgeon's diet consists mainly of immature aquatic insects sucked from the bottom. They also eat small snails, clams and bits of aquatic plants.

Spawning Habits — Spawn in late spring or early summer, usually at water temperatures of 65° to 70°F. They migrate upstream to spawn and randomly deposit their eggs over a rocky bottom, often in the swift water below a dam. No attempt is made to protect the eggs or young.

Age and Growth — Shovelnose sturgeon grow more slowly and have a shorter life span than other sturgeon. The maximum age is about 25 years.

Typical Length (inches) at Various Ages

Age	1	2	3	4	5	6	7	8	9
Length	8.8	13.3	16.5	17.2	18.2	20.4	21.9	23.1	24.1

Typical Weight (pounds) at Various Lengths (inches)

Length	16	19	22	25	28	31	34
Weight	.52	.89	1.4	2.1	3.0	4.3	6.4

World Record — 10 pounds, 12 ounces, caught in the Missouri River, Montana, in 1985.

32-inch shovelnose sturgeon — Minnesota River, Minnesota

Lake Sturgeon *(Acipenser fulvescens)*

Common Names — Rock sturgeon, black sturgeon, brown sturgeon, smoothback, and rubber-nose.

Description — The sides are brownish to slate gray, with no light-colored spots as on the white sturgeon. The long, cone-shaped snout has four barbels on the underside, about halfway between the mouth and the tip of the snout. The caudal peduncle is

24-pound lake sturgeon — St. Croix River, Minnesota

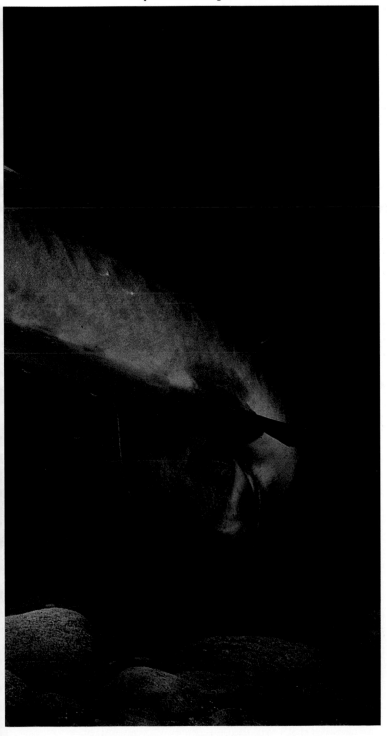

thicker than that of the shovelnose sturgeon, and is not covered with bony plates (photo at right). There is a spiracle at the top of the gill cover.

Table Quality — The rich, oily flesh is delicious when smoked. It can also be eaten fresh, but the taste is more like veal than fish.

Sporting Qualities — Because lake sturgeon are primarily bottom feeders, they are almost always caught on natural bait, particularly nightcrawlers, dead minnows, and cut bait. Veteran anglers use 20- to 50-pound-test line. Lake sturgeon are powerful fighters known for their leaping ability.

Habitat — Found only in large rivers and connecting lakes. The best rivers have long reaches not blocked by dams. Lake sturgeon usually inhabit areas with sand-gravel or rock bottoms. Their preferred temperature range is 60° to 65°F.

Food Habits — A lake sturgeon combs the bottom with its barbels, using its protractile mouth to suck in insect larvae, snails, small clams and crayfish. The heaviest feeding starts in the evening and continues until early morning.

Spawning Habits — Lake sturgeon do not become sexually mature until about age 20. They spawn in late spring or early summer, normally at water temperatures from 55° to 64°F. Before spawning, they thrash in the shallows and often leap completely out of the water. Spawning takes place in swift water, frequently in rapids below impassable falls.

Age and Growth — Males live as long as 55 years, females as long as 80. However, a 208-pound lake sturgeon caught in Lake of the Woods, Ontario, in 1953 was said to be 152 years old.

Typical Length (inches) at Various Ages

Age	1	10	20	30	40	50	60	70	80
Length	8.5	36.0	51.0	60.0	67.0	71.5	75.0	77.5	79.0

Typical Weight (pounds) at Various Lengths (inches)

Length	30	35	40	45	50	60	70
Weight	6.4	8.9	13.4	19.0	28.6	52.0	79.1

World Record — Unfortunately, all sturgeon species except the shovelnose are lumped together in the official records, so there is no specific record for lake sturgeon. However, a 193-pounder was caught in Mullet Lake, Michigan, in 1974. A 310-pounder was netted by commercial fishermen in Batchewana Bay, Lake Superior, in 1922.

White Sturgeon *(Acipenser transmontanus)*

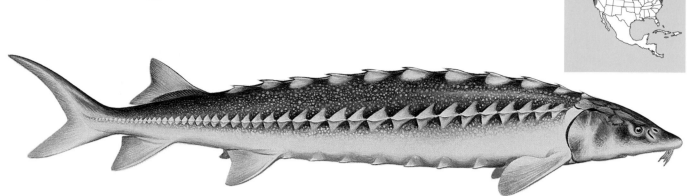

Common Names — Pacific sturgeon, Oregon sturgeon, Columbia sturgeon.

Description — Upper half of body grayish to brownish, usually speckled with white; lower half pale gray to white. The snout is short, somewhat flattened, and blunt when viewed from above. The barbels are closer to the tip of the snout than those of the lake sturgeon. There is a spiracle near the top of the gill cover.

Table Quality — The firm, white meat is good eating, and the eggs make excellent caviar.

Sporting Qualities — White sturgeon are the largest and most powerful fish in North American inland waters. A typical rig for white sturgeon consists of a heavy saltwater rod, 100-pound-test line, a ¾-pound sinker and a 12/0 hook. The best baits are cut fish, shrimp, and large clusters of nightcrawlers.

Habitat — Most white sturgeon are anadromous, spending the majority of their time in estuaries of large rivers along the Pacific coast and entering coastal rivers to spawn. But some spend their entire lives in the upper reaches of these rivers, hundreds of miles from the sea. White sturgeon are usually found in rivers with clean water and moderate current. Their preferred water temperature range is 65° to 70°F.

Food Habits — Although white sturgeon are primarily bottom feeders, they eat a wider variety of foods than other sturgeon. In addition to insect larvae, crustaceans and fish eggs, they feed on dead and live fish, frogs, and clams. A domestic cat was found in the stomach of one large sturgeon. They feed most heavily in the evening.

Spawning Habits — Spawn in late spring, usually at water temperatures of 50° to 60°F. The eggs are

Photo below: White sturgeon estimated at 1500 pounds, caught on a setline in the Snake River, Idaho, in 1898.

Photo on opposite page: 150-pound white sturgeon — South Bay, California

scattered over a rocky bottom with swift current, often below waterfalls or rapids. A female spawns only once every 5 to 10 years. White sturgeon move great distances on spawning migrations, and have been found as far inland as the Flathead River in Montana.

Age and Growth — The largest white sturgeon are probably over 100 years old. Growth is considerably faster in the southern part of their range.

Typical Length (inches) at Various Ages

Age	1	5	10	15	20	25	30	35	40
North	13.8	24.8	35.4	47.3	55.2	63.2	72.5	80.2	—
South	17.7	31.5	43.3	53.2	64.4	83.7	98.1	103.2	108.3

Typical Weight (pounds) at Various Lengths (inches)

Length	35	40	45	50	55	60	70	80	90
Weight	12.0	13.9	18.6	22.8	30.7	46.3	73.9	120.3	178.9

World Record — 468 pounds, caught in the Carquinez Straits, California, in 1983. Many larger white sturgeon have been caught commercially, including a 1387-pounder taken in the Fraser River, British Columbia, in 1897.

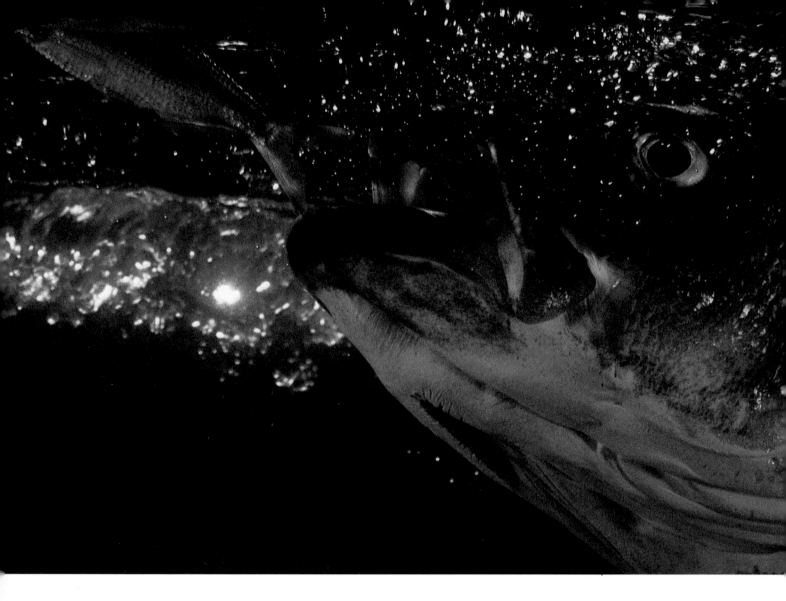

Temperate Bass Family

These highly aggressive gamefish are called temperate bass because of their preference for moderate water temperatures. They are sometimes called "true bass" to distinguish them from largemouth bass and other black bass, which actually are members of the sunfish family.

The temperate bass family *(Percichthyidae)* includes the white bass and yellow bass, which are strictly freshwater species; the white perch, which is found mainly in fresh water, but can be anadromous; and the striped bass, an anadromous species that has been successfully introduced to rivers and reservoirs in more than thirty states.

All temperate bass have two dorsal fins, numerous small teeth, and one or two sharp spines at the rear

edge of the gill cover. Most have rows of horizontal black stripes along the sides.

Unlike black bass, temperate bass are random spawners, not nest builders. They thrive in big rivers or in lakes connected to big rivers. They require flowing water for successful spawning.

Temperate bass have a strong schooling tendency. They feed in packs, surrounding schools of baitfish, herding them to the surface, then attacking them. The desperate baitfish leap out of the water as the bass slash at them. Gulls swoop down to grab the injured baitfish. The frenzied feeding may last only minutes, then the bass sound. But they soon appear in another location.

To pinpoint schools of feeding bass, experienced fishermen look for the circling gulls. This technique of following the active schools is called *jump fishing*.

Temperate bass have white, flaky meat that is good eating, but a bit on the oily side. It spoils quickly if not kept chilled. When you catch a temperate bass, immediately place it in a cooler with ice.

Striped bass attacking gizzard shad — Lake Ouachita, Arkansas

Temperate Bass Family — Species Identification Key

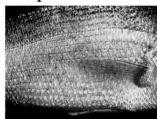 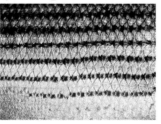

1 Sides plain or with faint streaks . . . .
 WHITE PERCH

Sides with definite dark stripes . . . .
 go to 2

2 Lower stripes broken in a line above anal fin . . . . .
 YELLOW BASS

Lower stripes unbroken, or broken in irregular pattern . .
 go to 3

3 Deep body; length less than 4 times depth . . . .
 WHITE BASS

Slender body; length more than 4 times depth . . . .
 STRIPED BASS

White Perch (*Morone americana*)

Common Names — Silver perch, bluenose perch and sea perch.

Description — The pale olive to silvery green sides lack the dark horizontal stripes present on other temperate basses. White perch also have a narrower tail. The deepest part of the body is at the front of the dorsal fin. On a white bass, the deepest part is near the middle of the back.

Hybrids — Known to hybridize with striped bass.

Table Quality — The firm, white meat is excellent eating.

Sporting Qualities — White perch are easily caught on worms, minnows, grass shrimp, small jigs, spinners, spoons, wet flies and streamers. But they spook even more easily than white bass, so anglers must keep their distance from the school. They wage a feisty but short battle.

Habitat — White perch can live in salt, brackish or fresh water. They thrive in inland lakes and reservoirs with expanses of warm, shallow water; in coastal rivers; and in lakes and ponds connected to estuaries. Preferred temperature range: 75° to 80°F.

Food Habits — White perch rely heavily on insects and crustaceans for food. Although they herd baitfish to the surface, especially on cloudy days, they feed this way less often than other temperate bass. In the evening, white perch can frequently be seen dimpling the surface as they take insects. Surface feeding often continues after dark. They seldom feed in winter.

Spawning Habits — Spawn in spring at water temperatures from 50° to 60°F. White perch swim up tributary streams and randomly deposit their eggs over gravel shoals or on sparse submerged vegetation. They do not guard the eggs or fry.

Age and Growth — White perch are slow-growing, but long-lived. The maximum age is about 17 years. Their high reproductive potential can create stunting problems if there are several good year-classes in a row.

Typical Length (inches) at Various Ages

Age	1	2	3	4	5	6	7	8	9
Length	3.6	5.5	6.9	7.7	8.5	9.4	10.2	10.9	11.5

Typical Weight (pounds) at Various Lengths (inches)

Length	7	8	9	10	11	12	13	14
Weight	.18	.26	.37	.52	.73	.93	1.5	2.1

World Record — 4 pounds, 12 ounces, caught in Messalonskee Lake, Maine, in 1949.

11-inch white perch — Rappahannock River, Virginia

Yellow Bass *(Morone mississippiensis)*

Common Names — Streaker, striper, brassy bass, gold bass.

Description — Yellow-gold sides with 6 or 7 dark horizontal stripes. The lower stripes are broken in a line above the front of the anal fin; on a white bass, the lower stripes may be broken, but the pattern is more irregular. The spiny and soft dorsal fins are joined at their bases. The lower jaw is slightly longer than the upper; on white bass, the lower jaw is considerably longer.

Hybrids — Known to hybridize with white bass.

Table Quality — The white, firm, flaky meat is very good eating, better than that of white bass.

Sporting Qualities — Although smaller than white bass, yellow bass are surprisingly tough fighters. They have similar pack-feeding habits, but are less likely to feed on the surface. The most effective lures and baits are jigs, flies, spoons, spinners, small plugs, minnows and worms.

Habitat — Most common in lakes with wide expanses of open water and few weeds, and in large rivers, including connecting backwaters and sloughs. Yellow bass prefer clear water, but will tolerate waters of low clarity. They prefer water temperatures of 75° to 80°F, although large yellow bass are some-times found in heated discharges where the temperature is 95°.

Food Habits — The diet is mainly fish. Yellow bass feed heavily in the shallows in early morning and in evening. They roam deep water in midday, feeding sporadically.

Spawning Habits — Spawn in spring, usually at water temperatures of 58° to 64°F. Like white bass, they swim up tributary streams to spawn and may deposit their eggs on the same sand-gravel shoals. They do not guard the eggs or fry.

Age and Growth — Yellow bass are slow-growing and short-lived. A few live to age 7, but the average is only 3 to 4.

Typical Length (inches) at Various Ages

Age	1	2	3	4	5
Length	3.7	7.7	8.7	9.5	10.7

Typical Weight (pounds) at Various Lengths (inches)

Length	6	7	8	9	10	11	12	13
Weight	.32	.39	.44	.51	.64	.83	1.1	1.3

World Record — 2 pounds, 4 ounces, caught in Lake Monroe, Indiana, in 1977. A 3-pound, 2-ounce yellow bass was netted in Lake Poygan, Wisconsin, in 1964.

10- to 11-inch yellow bass — Lake Chicot, Arkansas

White Bass *(Morone chrysops)*

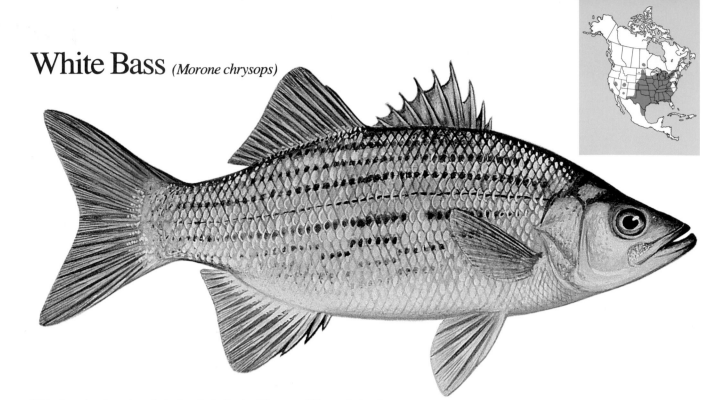

White bass herding gizzard shad — Lake Pepin, Minnesota/Wisconsin border

Common Names — Silver bass, striper, sand bass.

Description — The silvery sides have unbroken black stripes above the lateral line. Stripes below the lateral line are faint and often broken in an irregular pattern. The dorsal fins, unlike those of yellow bass, are not joined at the bases and the lower jaw is noticeably longer than the upper. There is a single patch of teeth at the base of the tongue; striped bass have two patches.

Hybrids — Known to hybridize naturally with yellow bass. Artificial white bass-striped bass hybrids (page 146) have been stocked in many southern states. They are called wipers, whiterocks, sunshine bass, or simply hybrids.

Table Quality — The firm, white meat is good eating, especially when the fatty, reddish meat is removed from the side of the fillet.

Sporting Qualities — Their aggressive nature combined with their schooling tendency make white bass one of the easiest fish to catch. During a feeding frenzy, they will strike practically any lure tossed into their midst, but you must be careful not to spook them. The best lures are jigs, spinners and spoons. Minnows will also work, but live bait is seldom needed. White bass are remarkably strong fighters for their size.

Habitat — The best populations are in large lakes connected to major river systems, and in big rivers with moderate current. They prefer clear water, but will tolerate murky conditions. Their preferred temperature range is 65° to 75°F.

Food Habits — White bass are primarily fish-eaters. They thrive on open-water baitfish like shad and emerald shiners, but will eat practically any fish available. Other foods include aquatic insect larvae and crustaceans. Although they feed most heavily around dawn and dusk, they also feed during midday and at night. Some feeding continues through the winter.

Spawning Habits — Spawn in spring, normally at water temperatures from 58° to 64°F. Spawning usually takes place in rivers but sometimes in shoal areas of lakes. In rivers, they run upstream to a dam or other barrier, then deposit their eggs in light current. After spawning, they abandon their eggs.

Age and Growth — Although white bass may live up to 10 years, few live beyond age 6. Females grow slightly faster than males.

Typical Length (inches) at Various Ages

Age	1	2	3	4	5	6
Length	5.3	10.3	12.3	13.3	14.0	14.7

Typical Weight (pounds) at Various Lengths (inches)

Length	9	10	11	12	13	15	17
Weight	.31	.44	.61	.81	1.1	1.7	2.6

World Record — 5 pounds, 14 ounces, caught in Kerr Lake, North Carolina, in 1986.

Striped Bass *(Morone saxatilis)*

Common Names — Striper, rockfish, linesides.

Description — The silvery sides have 7 or 8 unbroken horizontal stripes that are darker and more prominent than on a white bass. The body is more elongate, and there are two patches of teeth on the tongue, rather than one. A white bass has a single spine on the rear of the gill cover; a striper has two.

Hybrids — Known to hybridize naturally with white perch. Female striped bass are commonly bred with male white bass to produce a cross called a wiper, whiterock, sunshine bass, or simply hybrid.

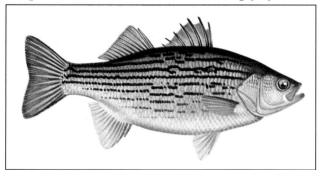

WIPER — Body depth intermediate between that of the white bass and striped bass; stripes broken both above and below lateral line. Stocked widely throughout striped bass range.

Table Quality — Excellent eating; the meat is white, firm and flaky.

Sporting Qualities — Its speed, power, and frenzied surface-feeding habits make the striped bass one of the most exciting freshwater sport fish. Stripers are usually caught by deep trolling with large plugs or jigs, or by drifting with live baitfish or cut bait. When "on the jumps," they can easily be caught by casting any type of artificial that resembles the baitfish they are chasing.

Habitat — Stripers are anadromous, entering freshwater streams to spawn. But many have been stocked in fresh water, mainly in large southern reservoirs.

They prefer relatively clear water with a good supply of open-water baitfish such as threadfin or gizzard shad. Their preferred water temperature range is 65° to 75°F.

Food Habits — Fish are the primary food, but stripers also eat crustaceans and a wide variety of insects and bottom organisms. Like other temperate bass, they move in packs, and all members of the pack tend to feed at the same time. Heaviest feeding is in early morning and in evening, but they feed sporadically throughout the day, especially when skies are overcast. Feeding slows when the water temperature drops below 50°F, but does not stop completely.

Spawning Habits — Spawn in spring, normally at water temperatures from 55° to 60°F. Stripers in reservoirs swim up tributary streams and often spawn below large dams. As many as fifty fish may spawn together, rolling and splashing in the shallows. The semi-buoyant eggs are deposited in light to moderate current. Moving water is needed to keep the eggs afloat until they hatch.

Age and Growth — Striped bass are fast-growing and long-lived. A 125-pounder caught by commercial netters off the Atlantic coast was estimated to be 29 to 31 years old.

Typical Length (inches) at Various Ages

Age	1	2	3	4	5	6	7	8	9
Length	9.3	16.7	21.1	24.4	27.5	29.8	31.9	33.7	34.9

Typical Weight (pounds) at Various Lengths (inches)

Length	18	21	24	27	30	33	36	39	42
Weight	2.8	4.3	6.3	9.1	12.3	15.9	20.2	26.4	36.8

World Record — Freshwater: 59 pounds, 12 ounces, caught in the Colorado River, Arizona, in 1977. Saltwater: 78 pounds, 8 ounces, caught off Atlantic City, New Jersey, in 1982.

Striped bass taking jig on casting float — Lake Lanier, Georgia

Herring Family

All members of the herring family are silvery, thin-bodied fishes that roam open water in large schools. They resemble whitefish (page 11), but have no adipose fin or lateral line. The scales are loosely attached, and form a saw-toothed keel along the belly.

Herring are primarily plankton-eaters. They have long, closely spaced gill rakers that are ideal for filtering tiny organisms from the water. Because herring can make use of this abundant food source, many waters support enormous populations.

In terms of total commercial value, the herring family (*Clupeidae*) surpasses any other family of fish. The family includes such marine species as sardines, pilchards and menhaden. Some members of the family, such as gizzard and threadfin shad, spend their entire lives in fresh water. Others, like American shad, hickory shad and blueback herring, are anadromous, entering fresh water only during the spawning period.

American and hickory shad are the family members of greatest interest to freshwater fishermen. During the spring spawning run, these species move into coastal rivers, sometimes in spectacular numbers. Although they do not feed after entering fresh water, they eagerly strike artificial lures.

Hickory shad taking shad dart — Rappahannock River, Virginia

Shad are considered good eating; the roe is eaten fresh and used for caviar. But the shad's popularity with fishermen is mainly due to its fighting ability. Hooked shad often cartwheel from the water several times, giving them the name "poor man's salmon."

Shad are native to the Atlantic coast. But in the late 1800s, American shad were stocked in the Sacramento River in California and in several other rivers along the Pacific coast. Today, American shad are found in coastal rivers from central California to southeastern Alaska.

Shad populations along the Atlantic coast have declined in recent years, as a result of pollution, loss of spawning habitat, and possibly acid rain. Some states have closed their rivers to shad fishing to protect the remaining broodstock.

Herring Family — Species Identification Key

1 Lower jaw projects beyond upper . . . .
HICKORY SHAD

Jaws of equal length, lower fits into notch in upper . . . .
AMERICAN SHAD

Hickory Shad (*Alosa mediocris*)

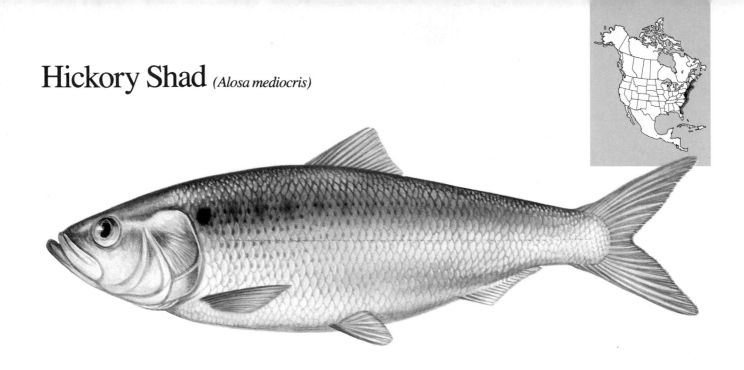

Common Names — Tailor shad, hick. Males are called buck shad, females roe shad.

Description — Silvery sides with large, loose scales; large, black spot behind the gill cover followed by several vague spots. The lower jaw, unlike that of American shad, projects well beyond the upper.

Table Quality — The eggs are delicious, but the meat is not as good as that of American shad.

Sporting Qualities — Although smaller than American shad, hickory shad are even more acrobatic fighters. They are generally caught on light spinning tackle with flies; small spoons; and small, flat-headed jigs called shad darts.

Habitat — Hickory shad are found in fresh water only during the spawning period and for a short time afterward. They swim up coastal rivers in early spring, then spread out in connecting backwaters and tributaries. By midsummer, most have returned to the sea or died. Hickory shad are seldom found at water temperatures less than the low 40s.

Food Habits — The diet consists of small fish, fish eggs, crabs, aquatic insects and squid.

Spawning Habits — Hickory shad begin running about two weeks earlier than American shad, usually entering rivers when the water temperature reaches 50° to 52°F. Males move in first, but as spawning time draws near, the percentage of females increases. Hickory shad prefer to spawn in small tributaries instead of the main river. Spawning activity usually peaks at water temperatures in the low 60s. The eggs are deposited at random, then abandoned.

Age and Growth — Hickory shad grow more slowly than American shad. The maximum age is about 10 years, but few live beyond age 6.

Typical Length (inches) at Various Ages

Age	1	2	3	4	5	6
Length	8.5	13.4	13.8	14.6	15.7	16.5

Typical Weight (pounds) at Various Lengths (inches)

Length	12	13	14	15	16	17	18
Weight	.65	.77	.92	1.1	1.4	1.7	2.1

World Record — No official record. A 2-pound, 13-ounce hickory shad was caught in Pitchkettle Creek, North Carolina, in 1974. Hickory shad up to 5 pounds have been caught in nets.

16-inch hickory shad — Nottoway River, Virginia

American Shad *(Alosa sapidissima)*

Common Names — White shad, Atlantic shad, common shad, and jack. As in hickory shad, the males are called buck shad and the females roe shad.

Description — Silvery sides with large, loose scales and a row of black spots behind the gill cover that become smaller and less colorful toward the tail. The upper and lower jaws are nearly equal in length; the lower fits neatly into a notch in the upper.

Table Quality — The white, flaky meat is good eating, either fresh or smoked. Shad-egg caviar is highly esteemed in some areas.

Sporting Qualities — When hooked on light tackle, shad wage a spectacular aerial battle. Most are caught on flies, small spoons, or shad darts.

Habitat — Found in fresh water only during the spawning run, when they swim up rivers along the Atlantic and Pacific coasts. They cannot tolerate cold water and avoid water temperatures below 41°F.

Food Habits — The diet consists mainly of plankton, which are filtered from the water by the gill rakers. Other foods include crustaceans, small fish and fish eggs.

Spawning Habits — American shad spawn as early as mid-November in Florida, and as late as July in Canada. Most spawning activity takes place at night, peaking at water temperatures in the mid-60s. The eggs are released near the surface and allowed to drift with the current. In the northern part of their range, American shad return to the sea after spawning; in the southern part, they die.

Age and Growth — Although shad live up to 11 years, few survive past age 7. First-time spawners generally weigh 3 to 5 pounds; repeat spawners 5 to 9 pounds. Females grow faster than males.

Typical Length (inches) at Various Ages

Age	1	2	3	4	5	6	7	8
Length	7.8	12.4	15.3	18.4	19.7	20.4	22.0	23.2

Typical Weight (pounds) at Various Lengths (inches)

Length	14	16	18	20	22	24	26
Weight	1.1	1.7	2.5	3.4	4.7	6.1	7.6

World Record — 11 pounds, 4 ounces, caught in the Connecticut River, Massachusetts, in 1986. In the early 1900s, 11- to 12-pounders were common, with an occasional fish up to 14 pounds.

19-inch American shad — Susquehanna River, Maryland

Cichlid Family

These tropical fish are found mainly in Africa and in South and Central America. One species, the Rio Grande perch, occurs naturally in southern Texas and has been stocked in other waters in the southern United States. It is the only cichlid species of much interest to fishermen.

Several species of tilapia, also members of the cichlid family *(Cichlidae),* have been stocked in southern states to control aquatic weeds or to reduce mosquito populations. In a few cases, they have been stocked as potential gamefish. But most states have discontinued tilapia stocking because the fish have proved more winter-hardy than previously thought, establishing permanent populations in some waters and competing with native sunfish and bass.

Besides tilapias, at least a dozen other cichlids have been stocked inadvertently in the United States. Species such as the oscar and firemouth have escaped from fish farms where they were being raised for aquarium purposes. Some of these species have established permanent populations in southern states. Most cichlids will not tolerate cold water, so they have not become established in the North.

Members of the cichlid family are easy to recognize. The lateral line is broken and offset, and there is only one opening, or *nare,* for each nostril. Other freshwater gamefish have a pair of nares for each nostril. Some cichlids have tremendous reproductive potential, spawning as often as ten times per year. This trait accounts for their popularity as aquarium fishes.

Rio Grande Perch *(Cichlasoma cyanoguttatum)*

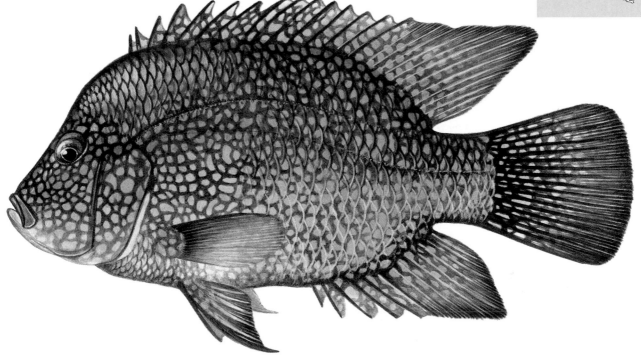

Common Names — Guinea perch, Rio Grande cichlid, Texas cichlid.

Description — The sides are bluish green to gray, with light speckles. The fins are long and flowing. The small mouth is well-equipped with sharp buckteeth. Mature males have a steeply humped forehead.

Table Quality — The white, flaky meat is considered very good eating. But the black lining of the body cavity should be removed to avoid a strong taste.

Sporting Qualities — Rio Grande perch are wary and not easily fooled by artificial lures. The best baits are small crayfish, worms and minnows. When caught on light tackle, they are strong, determined fighters with surprising stamina.

Habitat — Primarily river fish, Rio Grande perch are sometimes found in lakes connected to river systems. Like sunfish, they are normally found near weeds, submerged timber, riprap or other types of heavy cover. Rio Grande perch prefer a water temperature of about 80°F. They are intolerant of cold water and cannot survive temperatures below 55°. As a result, they often congregate around springs and heated discharges.

Food Habits — Common food items include aquatic insect larvae, small fish and fish eggs. Rio Grande perch are considered pests in some areas because they wage group attacks on the nests of bass and sunfish, consuming large numbers of eggs and fry.

Spawning Habits — Spawn in late spring or early summer at a water temperature of about 70°F. Males construct a nest, and both parents assist in guarding the young.

Age and Growth — Stream populations of Rio Grande perch are often stunted because of overcrowding, but where they have more space and a good food supply, 2-pounders are not unusual.

Typical Length (inches) at Various Ages

Age	1	2	3	4	5
Length	3.8	5.3	7.1	8.5	10.3

Typical Weight (pounds) at Various Lengths (inches)

Length	6	7	8	9	10	11	12
Weight	.23	.38	.59	.86	1.2	1.6	2.1

World Record — No official world record. Maximum size is about 3 pounds.

Index